CULTURES OF THE WORLD

EL SALVADOR

Erin Foley

MARSHALL CAVENDISH
New York • London • Sydney

Reference edition published 1997 by
Marshall Cavendish Corporation
99 White Plains Road
Tarrytown
New York 10591

© Times Editions Pte Ltd 1995

Originated and designed by
Times Books International, an imprint of
Times Editions Pte Ltd

Printed in Singapore

Library of Congress Cataloging-in-Publication Data:
Foley, Erin.
   El Salvador / Erin Foley.
     p. cm.—(Cultures Of The World)
   Includes bibliographical references and index.
   ISBN 1-85435-696-8 :
    1. El Salvador—Juvenile literature [1. El Salvador.]
I. Title. II. Title: Salvador. III. Series.
F1483.2.F65 1994
972.84—dc20   94–22567
             CIP
             AC

INTRODUCTION

DESPITE BEING BLESSED with a landscape of great beauty and fertility, and a people who have shown immense courage and spirit in the face of centuries of poverty and repression, El Salvador is a country that has experienced social, economic, and political problems of crisis proportions. Since colonial times, overpopulation and the scarcity of land have caused bitter fighting among its people and have affected every aspect of its development. A civil war that tore the country apart for 12 years and left some 75,000 people dead finally came to an end in 1992, and the process of rebuilding the country is under way. This book in the series *Cultures of the World* explores some of the factors that have contributed to El Salvador's turbulent past and takes a look at the lifestyle and culture of the people who call this lush but harsh country home.

CONTENTS

The vast majority of Salvadorans are of mixed Indian and Spanish descent. It is quite common to see the men wearing Western clothing and straw cowboy hats.

CONTENTS

Salvadoran firefighters and ambulance workers are easily spotted in their bright uniforms.

GEOGRAPHY

EL SALVADOR is a beautiful tropical land of ruined temples and ancient Mayan cities, volcanoes, mountain lakes, and Pacific black-sand beaches. Bordered by Guatemala to the west, Honduras to the north and east, and the Pacific Ocean to the south, the landscape is dominated by two parallel east-west mountain ranges that divide the country into its three main regions: the northern mountains and plain, the central region, and the southern coastal lowlands. El Salvador, only slightly larger than the state of Massachusetts, is the smallest country in Central America, but with over 650 people per square mile, it is more densely populated than any other mainland country in the Western Hemisphere.

Opposite: **A volcano towers majestically above the fertile plains outside San Salvador. The Indians called the San Salvador volcano Quetzaltepec, meaning "Mountain of the Quetzal Birds."**

Left: **A sweeping view of the Planes Renderos. A landscape of mountains interspersed with cities built on fertile plains is characteristic of the central region.**

The fertile lowland plains run in a narrow strip between the central highland region and the Pacific Ocean.

TOPOGRAPHY

It is hard to go anywhere in El Salvador without seeing a volcano. Scattered along the central region and interspersed with large, open plains is a chain of 20 volcanoes. These volcanoes, several of which are still active, have played a fundamental role in the history and development of the country. It is no accident that there is a major town at the base of each of the highest volcanoes—Santa Ana, San Vicente, San Miguel and San Salvador, all towering 6,000–8,000 feet above sea level. The volcanoes feed the plains below with a mixture of ash, lava, and sediment that has made the soil extremely fertile and able to support large concentrations of people for thousands of years. Though it makes up only a quarter of El Salvador's land, the region contains the country's biggest cities and most of the population.

The central highlands slope down to the south to form the narrow plains along the Pacific coast of El Salvador. The lowland soil is enriched by runoff from numerous small rivers that drain from the central highlands. Year-round high temperatures, in addition to heavy rains, ensure that the land is thick with foliage and good for agricultural cultivation.

In the broad plain and band of mountains north of the central region, agricultural conditions are less ideal. Lying only 1,300–2,000 feet above sea level, the plain suffers from poor drainage and acidic soil, while the steep slopes of the Sierra Madre mountains running along the border with Honduras have not been able to withstand the excessive clearing of forests and many years of agricultural overuse.

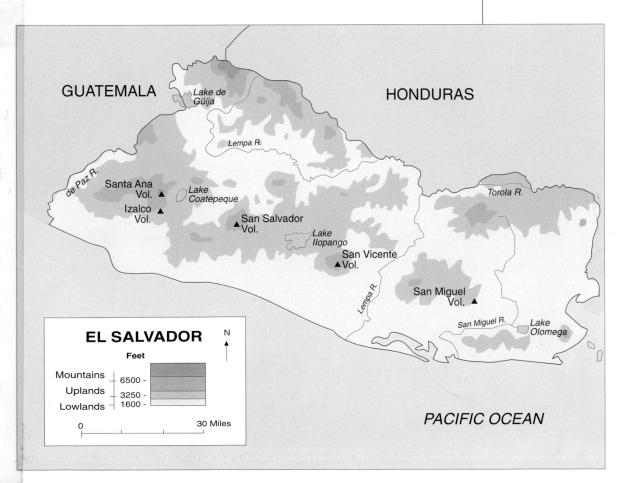

A LAND OF EARTHQUAKES AND VOLCANOES

El Salvador lies in a precarious position, right on the edge of three tectonic plates that cause frequent earthquakes and volcanic eruptions as they rub against each other. Although the movement of each plate is a barely perceptible six inches per year or less, over long periods of time it is enough to create chains of volcanic ridges and earthquake fault lines.

Earthquakes completely destroyed El Salvador's capital city twice, in 1756 and 1854, and badly damaged it three times this century. The most recent quake, in 1986, killed over a thousand people, and several buildings are still under reconstruction.

This building—one of many destroyed by the 1986 earthquake—now stands abandoned. Other, more important, buildings have since been restored.

THE IZALCO VOLCANO

In 1770, the Izalco volcano sprang up suddenly from a smoke-spouting hole in the ground and quickly grew to its current height of 7,828 feet. It exploded continuously over the next 187 years and was nicknamed the "Lighthouse of the Pacific"—at night, the molten lava running down its sides turned the volcano into a brightly glowing beacon that could be seen from miles out to sea. Now black and bare, Izalco is still classified as an active volcano, but has not erupted since 1966.

Volcanoes, too, have brought destruction to many Salvadoran towns. Although the twin-peaked San Salvador volcano, towering above the country's capital, has not erupted since 1917, San Miguel, the largest city in eastern El Salvador, has suffered 10 eruptions this century from its namesake volcano. Despite their destructive nature, volcanoes have been a blessing for El Salvador, making the soil extremely fertile and providing an alternative energy source that is still waiting to be fully tapped.

RIVERS AND LAKES

El Salvador has over 300 rivers, and the Lempa River is by far the most important. Entering El Salvador's northwest corner from Guatemala, the Lempa flows 145 miles across the country and down into the Pacific Ocean, draining about half of the country. The Lempa was once a major navigation and transportation route, but its importance now lies in its hydroelectric dams, the Cerrón Grande and the Cinco de Noviembre. The power harnessed by these dams helps El Salvador reduce its dependence on imported petroleum.

Many of the volcanoes in the central region have flooded to form beautiful lakes bordered by steep, green slopes. The largest of these, Lake Ilopango, just east of San Salvador, and Lake Coatepeque, in the west, are popular recreation spots for Salvadorans.

Lake Coatepeque, a clean, sparkling blue crater lake on the eastern slopes of the Santa Ana volcano, is a popular spot for swimming, boating, and fishing.

CLIMATE

Lying close to the equator, El Salvador experiences little variation in temperature throughout the year, and seasons are marked more by the difference in levels of rainfall. Temperatures do, however, vary between the three main regions, due to differences in altitude.

The rainy season, known as *invierno* ("in-vee-AIR-noh"), meaning "winter," lasts from May through October. During these months, it usually rains every evening, often in a downpour. June is the wettest month. The dry season, known as *verano* ("vay-RAH-noh"), or "summer," is from November through April, during which time much of El Salvador is dry and dusty. The hottest months are March, April, and May.

The moderate climate of the central region is typified by San Salvador: raised 2,156 feet above sea level, the capital's average temperature is 74°F, ranging from a minimum of 60–67°F during the night to a maximum of 86–94°F during the day. The coastal lowlands are usually much hotter, with an average of 83°F and high humidity. Northern mountain areas average only 64°F, and temperatures occasionally drop to near freezing.

The cool, clear springs at Los Chorros, a park near San Salvador, provide a welcome respite from El Salvador's tropical heat.

FLORA AND FAUNA

Large-scale deforestation and agriculture have destroyed much of El Salvador's animal and plant life. Rich stands of ebony, cedar, and mahogany once covered much of the country, but they have been cleared to open up land for crop cultivation and to provide valuable wood for export. Only six percent of the country remains forested, and trees are still being cut down without being replaced. The years of exploitation have taken their toll on the soil, which is badly eroded, especially on the slopes of the northern mountains. Formerly abundant species of cats and monkeys have disappeared, and although deer, pumas, coyotes, tapirs, and peccaries (wild pigs) can still be found in the mountains, the destruction of much of their habitat has decreased their numbers.

Crocodiles can be found in some of El Salvador's rivers.

Palm trees and tropical fruit trees, such as coconut, mango, and tamarind, flourish in the hot, humid coastal plains, as do armadillos, iguanas, and snakes. Bird life includes wild ducks, white and royal herons, blue jays, and the urraca—a grey-headed, blue-breasted bird noted for its call, which resembles a scoffing laugh. Turtles and a wide variety of fish populate El Salvador's rivers and coastal waters.

MONTECRISTO CLOUD FOREST

At the 7,931-foot summit of Montecristo Mountain, near where the borders of El Salvador, Guatemala, and Honduras converge, lies El Trifinio, an international nature reserve protected by all three countries. Inside El Trifinio is the Montecristo Cloud Forest, the last vestige of rainforest in El Salvador and one of the few remaining cloud forests in Central America.

Leaves and flowers of El Salvador's national tree, the maquilishuat.

At Montecristo, the oak and laurel trees grow almost 100 feet tall, their branches and leaves intertwining to form a canopy that is impenetrable to sunlight. With 100 percent humidity and 80 inches of rain a year, the forest is constantly dripping wet, creating an ideal habitat for a wide variety of exotic plants, including mushrooms, orchids, lichens, mosses, and ferns. Some ferns grow more than 25 feet tall.

The cloud forest's protected microclimates also support an abundance of animal life not found elsewhere in El Salvador: spider monkeys, two-fingered anteaters, porcupines, spotted and hooded skunks, pumas, red and grey squirrels, wild pigs, coyotes, and opossums. Montecristo is home to at least 87 species of birds, including woodpeckers, nightingales, hummingbirds, white faced quails, striped owls, and green toucans.

The pyramid at Tazumal is thought to have been built in A.D. 980, at the height of the Mayan civilization in Central America. The pyramid has now been restored.

MAYAN RUINS

Archeologists have unearthed remains of ancient cities at Tazumal and San Andrés proving that the Maya, one of the world's great civilizations, lived here 7,000 years ago.

Tazumal, meaning "pyramid where the victims were burned" in the Mayan language Quiché, has a stepped pyramid as well as the remains of a large courtyard attesting to the ritual ball games of the Maya. The clay vessels, ritual ornaments, and sculptures found at the ruins demonstrate that the Indians engaged in trade with people as far away as Panama and Mexico. Tazumal has been only partially excavated, as much of the 10 square mile site is buried under the present-day town of Chalchuapa.

San Andrés, just west of San Salvador, was inhabited by a succession of Maya, Aztec, and Pipil Indians. Pottery, grinding stones, and flint have been found, and a courtyard has been excavated. The ruins have been nicknamed the *Ruinas de la Campana de San Andrés*, or "The Ruins of the Bell of San Andrés," because of the bell-shaped pyramids that have yet to be excavated.

Archeologists have discovered the presence of another ruined city at Joya de Cerén. The new site is believed to be one of the best-preserved prehistoric villages in Latin America and has been billed as "the Pompeii of Central America."

CITIES

For thousands of years, most of the people of El Salvador have chosen to live in the central plains where the soil is rich and fertile. Spanish colonial settlements, many of them built on the sites of ancient Indian cities, have now become the principal cities of San Salvador, Santa Ana, and San Miguel.

San Salvador, the capital, now bustles with over 1.5 million people—more than a quarter of the country's total population—in its center and suburbs. Following a pattern that has been repeated in cities the world over, San Salvador has been a magnet for Salvadorans fleeing poverty and warfare in rural areas, but has failed to meet the increased demand for housing and jobs. The city reflects the huge gap between rich and poor in El Salvador: established, luxurious neighborhoods overlook the city from the surrounding hilltops, while shantytowns of makeshift huts made out of cardboard, tin, or mud cram the outskirts.

Santa Ana, with a population of 452,000, is the transportation hub and center for the western half of the country; its Indian name Cihuatehuacán means "place of holy women."

San Miguel, a lively market town of 380,000, attracts people from all over the eastern half of the country.

San Salvador's heavy traffic spews thick, black pollution, which is trapped in an air pocket formed by the city's location in a valley surrounded by hills.

17

HISTORY

THE HISTORY of El Salvador stretches back thousands of years, to a time when Indians inhabited the region, living off the fertile soil and honing their knowledge of astronomy and mathematics. The Spanish Conquest in 1528 put an end to a life of subsistence farming for the Indians and marked the beginning of a turbulent era that continues today. Claiming the land for themselves, the colonialists pushed the Indians into servitude and poverty, and established the power of the oligarchy and the Catholic Church. Even after independence, the landowning elite, the Catholic Church, and the military worked hand in hand to protect their power and wealth. Despite often brutal repression at the hands of the military, the peasants continued to fight against their landlessness and poverty. In 1980, rebellion escalated into civil war. Only since peace was negotiated in 1992, bringing promises of major economic and social reform, has El Salvador been able to look forward to a brighter future.

Left: **Rebel leaders Joaquín Villalobos and Shafik Hándel at a press conference at the end of the civil war that saw the death of about 75,000 Salvadorans.**

Opposite: **Guerrillas bombed San Salvador's Tower of Democracy building, nicknamed Tower of Hypocrisy, at least twice during the war.**

ANCIENT CIVILIZATIONS

The true discoverers of the Americas were a group of Asian tribes who crossed over the Bering Strait to North America, starting around 40,000 B.C., and slowly migrated southward into Central and South America. The Olmecs, arriving in about 2000 B.C., were the first ancient civilization to leave their mark in Central America. Although much about their culture remains a mystery, they are known to have made technical, artistic, and scientific advances that laid the groundwork for the extraordinary cultural achievements of the Maya.

The Maya flourished from about 400 B.C. until about A.D. 1000. Guatemala was the center of their civilization, but they also lived in the western half of El Salvador. The Maya built their economy around agriculture, cultivating an enormous variety of plants. In addition to corn, they raised several types of beans, gourds, squashes, and other produce unknown in Europe at the time, such as tomatoes, peanuts, green peppers, cacao, vanilla, chili peppers, avocados, and pineapples.

As they developed more and more advanced systems of producing food, the Maya were able to devote more time and energy to developing their skills in the arts and sciences. In hieroglyphic writing, astronomy, and mathematics, the Mayan Indians were far ahead of any other people in the New World.

The Mayan civilization suddenly and mysteriously collapsed around A.D. 980. It was at this time that the Toltec empire reached its peak of power and prosperity. The Toltecs disappeared around the 12th century, opening the way for the Nahuatl-speaking Chichimec tribes. The Aztecs were among the Chichimec tribes to move in from the north to occupy the region.

The Pipil, a Nahua people closely related to the Aztecs, are thought to

By the time the Spanish arrived in Central America in the 16th century, the Indians had made agricultural advances far beyond those of Europe.

have migrated south from Mexico around the 12th century and settled in an area covering parts of what is now El Salvador and Guatemala. They called their new land Cuscatlán, or "Land of the Jewel."

By the time of the Spanish Conquest in the 16th century, there was a large class of artisans and specialists, including carpenters, potters, stonemasons, hunters, dancers, and musicians, who enjoyed a position of high honor and responsibility. Society was highly organized, with a strict hierarchy (priests, warriors, and bureaucrats occupied the top rungs of the ladder) and a well developed government and judicial system. Books made from bark were used to record calendars, astronomical tables, taxes, dynastic history, and court records. Religion was the major focus of Nahua culture and priests played a key role in the daily life of the people.

The Olmec Boulder in Chalchuapa is evidence of Olmec presence in what is now El Salvador. Monumental stone carvings and sculptures were important elements of Olmec culture.

A statue of Christopher Columbus outside the National Palace stands as a symbol of the Spanish conquest of Central America.

THE SPANISH CONQUEST

Hungry for gold and silver, the Spanish conquistador Pedro de Alvarado first attacked Cuscatlán in June 1524. The Pipil Indians proved to be formidable opponents, however, and Alvarado's men were forced to withdraw to Guatemala. The Spaniards later returned and finally succeeded in defeating the Pipil in 1528. They renamed the small colony El Salvador ("the Savior"), but were disappointed to find very little gold or silver.

The Spanish settlers who followed realized that El Salvador's wealth lay in the richness of its soil and the size of its Indian population. Knowing that huge profits could be reaped by cultivating single crops for export, the Spanish Crown took the land away from the Indians and parceled it out to a handful of settlers. These 14 landowning families—*Los catorce grandes*, or "14 Families," as they came to be called—created enormous plantations to grow cacao (for chocolate), indigo (a natural dye) and, later, coffee. They then looked to the Indians for labor.

The Indians, deprived of their livelihood, found themselves forced to work on the plantations under slave-like conditions, serve in the Spanish army, and pay monetary tributes to the local authorities. Many Indians rose up in protest, but their machetes were no match for the Spaniards' guns.

INDEPENDENCE

The colonialists in Central America declared their independence from Spain on September 15, 1821. Two years later, they attempted to create a confederation of states—similar to the United States of America—by forming a union called the United Provinces of Central America, but ideological differences between the state governments caused the confederation to fall apart. El Salvador finally declared its independence as a sovereign country in January 1841.

Independence failed to bring about any improvement to the everyday lives of most Salvadorans. The government eliminated the last communal Indian farms and introduced "antivagrancy" laws that prevented Indians from looking for new land and forced them to work for the large landowners. The country's power and wealth remained concentrated in the hands of the landowning "14 Families." Strongly supported by the Catholic Church, this closely knit group exercised their control through the government and a newly created National Guard, and thus managed to preserve their position and suppress any dissent.

The "14 Families," now grown to about 200, still control about 60% of El Salvador's land and more than half of its wealth.

THE AQUINO UPRISING

In 1833, Anastasio Aquino, an Indian whose brother had been imprisoned by a wealthy planter, led the most famous of many revolts against the Spanish colonialists, rallying thousands of Indian and *mestizo* peasants with the cry "Land for those who work it!" The strength and unity of the uprising posed a serious threat to the government, but the Indians were soon defeated by the heavy cannons of the government forces. Aquino was captured and executed, but he is remembered as a national hero today.

LA MATANZA

La Matanza, or "The Slaughter," of 1932 is one of the great tragedies in El Salvador's history and was an early sign of the lengths to which the oligarchy was prepared to go in order to preserve their wealth and power.

1931 was a time of economic hardship: the Great Depression abroad caused a sharp drop in prices for coffee, El Salvador's main export crop, and the plight of the already poor Indian peasants became even worse when wages and employment levels tumbled further. The creation of a Salvadoran Communist party by university student Agustín Farabundo Martí made the establishment nervous. In December 1931, the military deposed the reformist president, Arturo Araújo, and installed General Maximiliano Hernández Martínez, nicknamed El Brujo, or "the warlock," in his place.

Farabundo Martí started agitating for change and in January 1932 led Indians in several rural areas to rise up against the system of land ownership that had caused their poverty. Military forces executed Farabundo Martí three days before the uprising actually began, and quickly suppressed the rebel forces. But they did not stop there: intent on deterring any further protest in the future, government soldiers systematically killed thousands of Indian peasants who had not even participated in the uprising. By the end of "The Slaughter," about 30,000 Indians were dead.

Rebel leader Agustín Farabundo Martí's name lives on in the guerrilla group Frente Farabundo Martí de Liberación Nacional (FMLN), which has continually fought for a fairer distribution of wealth.

REBELLION AND REPRESSION

La Matanza did not succeed in preventing the continued and mounting pressure for political and economic reform. In the 1960s, representatives from the government, the opposition, and labor and business groups recommended the large-scale redistribution of land to the peasants. Conservative members of the government, the military, and the landowning elite,

however, refused to have anything to do with reform. The conservative forces reasserted their power by rigging the presidential election in 1972; when it appeared that the victor was José Napoleón Duarte, the moderate, reformist candidate from the Christian Democratic Party, they arrested, tortured, and exiled him.

Social unrest and political violence began to increase: guerrilla groups grew larger and bolder, and mass demonstrations and strikes became more frequent, all of which prompted increasingly brutal suppression by the military against anyone who was even suspected of being a "subversive." Death squads, funded by the oligarchy and organized by the military, kidnapped, tortured, and killed thousands of civilians, especially in the cities, who supported or were thought to support reform. The victims, snatched away suddenly and usually never seen alive again, came to be known as *Los desaparecidos*, or "the disappeared," as knowledge of their abduction, whereabouts, and fate was routinely denied by the authorities.

Thousands of Salvadoran civilians were tortured and killed by military and paramilitary forces during the 1980s.

THE EL MOZOTE MASSACRE

In early December 1981, the Salvadoran army's U.S.-trained Atlacatl Battalion, led by Lieutenant Colonel Domingo Monterrosa Barrios, carried out one of the largest massacres in modern Latin American history. In the mountain villages of El Mozote, Los Toriles, and La Joya near the Honduran border, Monterrosa and his men killed an estimated 1,000 civilians.

The massacre was part of an army operation, called Operation Rescue, to break the guerrilla strongholds in the northern mountain region of Morazán. Although El Mozote itself was not reputed to be a guerrilla town (most of the inhabitants were born-again Christians who were known to be anti-Communist), it was in the heart of what the army referred to as the "Red Zones." Soldiers carried out a "sweep" of the entire area; in some villages they executed only people they believed to be guerrilla sympathizers, but in El Mozote and surrounding hamlets they killed everyone. Men were decapitated, women were shot, young women and girls were raped and then shot, and children and babies were impaled, hung, shot, crushed with rifle butts, or slashed with machetes.

Although eyewitness reports soon reached the outside world, Salvadoran and U.S. officials denied that a massacre had taken place. The U.S. Congress was in the middle of debating whether to cut off aid to El Salvador, and the Republican administration needed to be able to claim that the Salvadoran government was making progress on human rights in order to be able to continue its policy of fighting Communism in El Salvador.

It was not until after the peace accord was signed 11 years later that the truth was finally established. A team from the world-renowned Argentine Forensic Anthropology Unit began digging in El Mozote and found hundreds of skulls, bones, and U.S. weapons and ammunition. The U.N.-appointed Truth Commission concluded that a massacre of over a thousand civilians had indeed occurred, and that the Atlacatl Battalion was responsible.

CIVIL WAR

Late 1979 and early 1980 was a crucial time in El Salvador's history. A coup led by reformist young officers resulted in the setting up of a coalition junta that pledged sweeping land reforms and an end to repression. José Napoleón Duarte returned from exile, and hopes for a new and improved El Salvador ran high. Inevitably, however, the junta faced strong opposition from both the guerrillas and the rightwing factions of the army, and death squad activity increased. Catholic priests and nuns began to speak out against the repression and the poverty, and they too became government targets. Archbishop Oscar Arnulfo Romero was assassinated on March 24, 1980 while saying Mass. Later that year, four churchwomen, including three nuns, were killed by the military as they were driving through the countryside. No one was prosecuted for the crimes. Full-scale civil war between the rebels and government forces erupted and the United States, fearing the spread of Communism in Central America, donated large amounts of economic and military aid to El Salvador. Duarte was elected president in 1984, but his inability to bring an end to the fighting, coupled with corruption within his party, caused his downfall. The rightwing ARENA party, led by Alfredo Cristiani, won the 1989 election. The turmoil and destruction caused by the ongoing war affected every aspect of life in El Salvador, and by the late 1980s, the country's social, economic, and political problems had reached crisis proportions.

Paramedics attend to a wounded soldier.

THE ROLE OF THE UNITED STATES

U.S. policy in El Salvador stretches back several decades. Seeking to protect its strategic interests in Central America, the United States has supplied large amounts of military and economic aid to help the Salvadoran government fight the rebel forces. Although it stopped short of sending American combat troops, the United States played a significant role in training Salvadoran army battalions, and it supplied the latest in weaponry—M16s, M60 machine guns, 90-mm recoilless rifles, and 60- and 81-mm mortars. A group of 10 American advisors were working with the Salvadoran Atlacatl Battalion at the time of the El Mozote massacre.

Although Democratic President Jimmy Carter threatened to cut off aid in response to human rights abuses in El Salvador, he was not prepared to take the blame for any advance of Communism that a rebel victory might bring, and so concentrated instead on using military aid and social programs to encourage democracy in El Salvador. His attempts to break the oligarchy and redistribute wealth, however, only strengthened the repressive Salvadoran armed forces.

When Ronald Reagan came to power, the Republican administration called for a strengthening of U.S. policy and vowed to "draw the line" against Communism in El Salvador. Around the time that initial reports of the El Mozote massacre were making front-page news in the United States, military and economic aid to El Salvador was increased. By the mid-1980s, the U.S. government was sending $1.2 million a day to the Salvadoran government to help it fight the war. The Republicans argued that the tolerance of human rights atrocities was deplorable but necessary, because they believed a Communist victory was by far the worst disaster that could befall human rights in Central America. Preserving the Salvadoran government and helping it win the war were of paramount importance.

The proliferation of anti-U.S. graffiti is evidence that many Salvadorans saw the role of the United States as interventionist and resented it. "Be a patriot, kill a Yankee" and "Imperialists, get out of El Salvador" are typical slogans (see photo above).

PEACE

In the late 1980s, international pressure to end the war increased, and the end of the Cold War made it harder for the United States to justify continuing its military aid. Negotiations between the government and the FMLN guerrillas began in September 1989, but were disrupted by further violence. The FMLN attempted a "final offensive" to overthrow the Salvadoran government, but failed to rouse enough popular support. The army, for their part, broke into the Catholic university in San Salvador and murdered six Jesuit priests, their housekeeper, and her daughter.

The Jesuit killings shocked international observers as well as people in El Salvador. U.S. aid was halted, prompting the Salvadoran government to reopen peace negotiations; the FMLN, after their failed "final offensive," also agreed to talk. Both sides invited the United Nations to mediate, and after two years of hard negotiating, a peace agreement was finally signed in January 1992. Under the terms of the agreement, the FMLN agreed to lay down its arms in return for wide-ranging reforms, including land redistribution, a substantial decrease in the size and role of the armed forces, and a purge of the worst human rights offenders from the army officer corps.

Implementing the agreement has proved difficult and slow. The FMLN did demobilize its forces on December 15, 1992, and several army battalions were dissolved well ahead of the target date of mid-1994. Nevertheless, the government was slow to dismiss human rights offenders, is behind schedule on deploying a civilian police force, and has yet to make any real progress on land reform. The FMLN, meanwhile, has attracted criticism since a number of arms caches belonging to them were discovered in the region.

The signing of the peace accord on January 16, 1992, at Chapultepec Castle in Mexico marked the end of the most violent period in El Salvador's history.

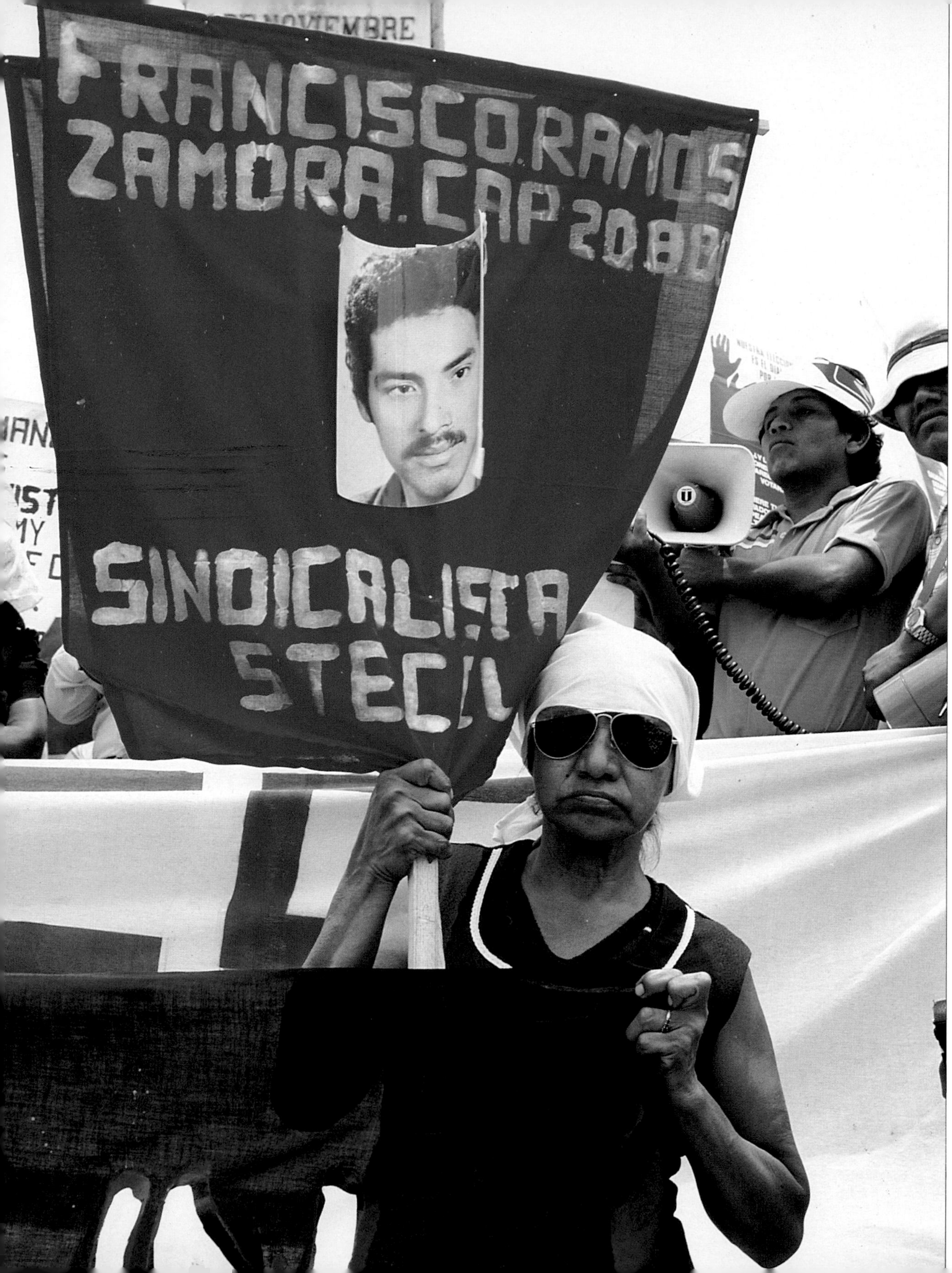
FRANCISCO RAMOS
ZAMORA. CAP 20.800
SINDICALISTA
STECEL

GOVERNMENT

THE ARMED FORCES have long dominated political life in El Salvador, despite a constitution that describes the country as a democratic republic with an elected president, a U.S.-style Supreme Court system, and voting rights for every Salvadoran over the age of 18. The oligarchy and the military have regularly set democracy aside, using coups, rigged elections, and repression to maintain their power and prestige. Government repression was particularly brutal during the 12-year civil war that ended in 1992. During this period, tens of thousands of ordinary Salvadorans were harassed, tortured, or killed by government forces for simply exercising their right to speak out in favor of reform; killings by paramilitary death squads went not only unpunished but unacknowledged by the courts. With the 1992 peace agreement came a framework for reforming the judicial system, the electoral process, the armed forces, and the police. Many of these changes have been highly controversial and difficult to implement, but progress has been made despite long delays.

Left: **Children campaign for the ARENA party's candidate. Excitement surrounded the 1994 national elections, the first "open" elections in El Salvador's history.**

Opposite: **Women banded together into the group COMADRES, or "Mothers of the Disappeared," and staged demonstrations since the 1980s, demanding to know what had happened to abducted relatives.**

NATIONAL GOVERNMENT

The government is divided into three branches: the executive, the legislative assembly, and the judiciary.

THE EXECUTIVE BRANCH This branch, consisting of the president, the council of ministers, and the undersecretaries of state, is responsible for preparing the budget, managing the armed forces and the security forces, and directing foreign relations. Presidential elections are held every five

The National Palace in San Salvador is the administrative center of the executive branch of government. The building had to be restored after it was seriously damaged in the 1986 earthquake.

years and presidents cannot serve more than one term of office in a row. Every presidential candidate must belong to a legally recognized political party and needs an absolute majority of the votes in order to win.

THE LEGISLATIVE ASSEMBLY The 64 members of the single-chamber Legislative Assembly are also popularly elected, serving renewable three-year terms. The assembly controls taxes, sanctions the budget, and ratifies or rejects international treaties.

THE JUDICIARY The most important judicial institution is the Supreme Court of Justice. Composed of the constitutional, the civil, and the criminal chambers, the Supreme Court rules on the constitutionality of laws and acts as the last level of appeal in civil and criminal cases.

Anti-government graffiti in the Plaza Libertad, San Salvador. It reads "Cristiani, President of the Death Squads." Alfredo Cristiani and his rightwing ARENA party governed El Salvador from 1989 to 1994.

LOCAL GOVERNMENT

El Salvador is divided into 14 administrative departments (equivalent to states in the United States), which in turn are divided into 261 municipalities (equivalent to counties). Each department has a governor and a substitute governor who are appointed by the government.

The citizens of each municipality directly elect their own municipal council, composed of a mayor, a legal representative, and two or more council members, depending on the population of the municipality.

MILITARY RULE

From independence until the peace agreement in 1992, politics in El Salvador has been dominated by the armed forces and the civilian oligarchy. The military protected the wealth and privileges of the oligarchy, while boosting their own status and power. Even in the 1980s, when the military ceded direct rule to civilian governments, they continued to play an influential role in the running of the country.

The officer corps developed its own criteria for advancement and rewards that had more to do with politics than military ability. Those who graduated together from the Gerardo Barrios Military Academy would be promoted together, acquiring wealth and power along the way, and defending each other vigorously against external criticism.

Since the 1992 peace accord, the hold of the military may finally be breaking, as 102 army officers who were named the worst abusers of human rights during the civil war have either resigned or been removed from office. Although President Alfredo Cristiani has attracted criticism for failing to replace General Ponce, the former minister of defense, with a civilian, the appointment of Colonel Humberto Corado Figueroa marks a clear end to the influence of the Tandona, the 1966 graduating class that ran the armed forces during much of the civil war.

REFORM

The 1992 peace agreement included as conditions a number of judicial and political reforms designed to protect civilians from human rights abuses and limit the role of the military. The main requirements of the accord were:

• To create a civilian-controlled police force to replace the military-controlled National Police (PN). The government has established the National Civilian Police (PNC). However, poor funding and a lack of commitment have delayed the transition from the PN to the PNC—by January 1994, only four out of 14 departments were policed by the PNC.

• To create an intelligence service independent of the armed forces and directly accountable to the president. A new agency, the State Intelligence Agency, has been set up to replace the old National Intelligence Department; it is directly accountable to the president, and its activities are supervised by the Legislative Assembly.

• To reduce the number of armed forces personnel from 53,000 to 22,000. Nineteen counter-insurgency units and five rapid-response battalions were dissolved in late 1992 and early 1993, ahead of schedule.

• To purge the highest levels of the armed forces of 102 officers named by the Ad Hoc Commission as violators of human rights. Although President Alfredo Cristiani removed 87 of these men from office by the December 31, 1992 deadline, it took international pressure for action to be taken against the remaining 15 officers six months later.

• To guarantee full political freedom for the FMLN. The FMLN was recognized as a legal political party in December 1992, and participated in its first election in 1994.

THE TRUTH COMMISSION REPORT

The 1992 peace agreement called for a U.N.-appointed Truth Commission to investigate the most serious human rights violations of the war period and publicize its conclusions. In March 1993, the commission released its report, entitled "From Madness to Hope: the 12-Year Civil War in El Salvador," containing the results of their investigations.

They found that Roberto d'Aubuisson, former leader of the ARENA party, ordered the killing of Archbishop Oscar Arnulfo Romero in 1980; that General René Emilio Ponce, then minister of defense, ordered the killings of six Jesuit priests in 1989; and that the Atlacatl Battalion was responsible for the massacre of 1,000 civilians at El Mozote. The report also revealed abuses carried out by the FMLN during the war, and accused the United States of ignoring Salvadoran human rights abuses in its determination to prevent an FMLN victory.

Although the FMLN and church and human rights groups welcomed the report, the Salvadoran government reacted negatively to it, denying many of the accusations. A few days after the release of the report, the government issued an amnesty for all those involved in the perpetration of atrocities.

POLITICAL PARTIES

El Salvador has eight legally recognized political parties, several of which were created since 1992.

ARENA (Nationalist Republican Alliance): The ruling rightwing party founded in 1981 and now headed by Arnando Calderón Sol.

PDC (Christian Democratic Party): This moderate party currently holds the second largest number of seats in the Legislative Assembly and is led by Fidel Chávez Mena.

CD (Democratic Convergence): A coalition of small leftwing parties led by Rubén Zamora, a respected intellectual and vice-president of the Legislative Assembly.

FMLN (Farabundo Martí National Liberation Front): The former guerrilla group, recognized as a legal political party in 1992.

PCN (National Conciliation Party): A small conservative party tied to the armed forces.

MU (Unity Movement): This evangelical party formed in 1993 is headed by Jorge Martínez Menéndez.

MAC (Authentic Christian Movement): An evangelical party formed as an offshoot of PDC and led by Julio Adolfo Rey Prendes.

MSN (National Solidarity Movement): An evangelical party led by Edgardo Rodríguez Engelhard.

The constitution bars Alfredo Cristiani (above), who has been president of El Salvador since 1989, from running for a consecutive term. His ARENA party named Arnando Calderón Sol as its candidate for the 1994 elections.

THE 1994 ELECTIONS

The 1994 presidential, legislative, and municipal elections were significant in many ways. It is rare for all three elections to be held concurrently, but more importantly, they were the first to be held since civil war ended and the first to be open to the FMLN guerrilla group, now recognized as a legal party. Three new evangelical parties also took part in the elections. The elections were seen as a test of the ability of a civilian government to hold

A crowd gathers to listen to a speaker in San Salvador's Central Plaza.

PEOPLE IN POLITICS, PAST AND PRESENT

AGUSTÍN FARABUNDO MARTÍ: Founder of El Salvador's Communist party; organized two-day farm workers' revolt in 1932, which provoked the retaliatory murder of thousands of peasants by the military. The FMLN guerrilla movement and political party were named for him.

GENERAL MAXIMILIANO HERNÁNDEZ MARTÍNEZ: Seized control of the government in a military coup in 1931; ordered the *matanza* in response to the 1932 farm workers' revolt.

JOSÉ NAPOLEÓN DUARTE: Former leader of the moderate Christian Democratic Party. He was tortured and exiled to Venezuela by government forces in 1972, but later returned to El Salvador and served as president from 1984 to 1989.

ROBERTO D'AUBUISSON: Founder of the rightwing ARENA party, he also set up the country's notorious death squads. He is alleged to have planned the 1980 assassination of Archbishop Romero.

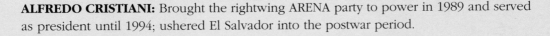

ALFREDO CRISTIANI: Brought the rightwing ARENA party to power in 1989 and served as president until 1994; ushered El Salvador into the postwar period.

RUBÉN ZAMORA: (Pictured above.) Leftwing intellectual and vice-president of the Legislative Assembly. He ran for president in the 1994 elections with the support of the two leftwing parties, the Democratic Convergence and the FMLN.

its own against the military. Prior to the elections, administrative problems were reported, and there were alleged to be irregularities among voter registrations (many known FMLN supporters found themselves without a vote) as well as an increase in violence against political figures. The March election was inconclusive. In the May run-off election, Armando Calderón Sol of the incumbent ARENA party won with a 68% majority. Although it lost the election, FMLN won 22 of the 84 seats in the National Assembly, firmly establishing itself as the major opposition party.

ECONOMY

THE SALVADORAN ECONOMY has been based on agriculture for thousands of years, but when the Spanish colonialists pushed the Indians off their small communal farms and used the land to grow cash crops, they made a fundamental change to the economy. Cash crops were indeed a success, and the later diversification into a greater variety of crops and into manufacturing ensured continued high levels of economic growth and extreme wealth for the few large landowners. The uneven distribution of wealth resulted in long-term political instability and, eventually, civil war. The war, in turn, had a major impact on the economy, causing a massive outflow of money, the destruction of much of the country's infrastructure, a decrease in exports, investment, and consumption, and even higher levels of unemployment. Since 1992, peace has brought generous foreign aid and the return of capital from abroad, restoring economic growth—at least in the short term.

In 1993, economic growth returned to its pre-civil war level of five percent but inflation and unemployment remained high.

Opposite: **A fisherman cuts an eel in the coastal town of La Libertad. The fishing industry has expanded considerably over the past few decades.**

Left: **A bus in San Salvador is the target of economic sabotage. Rebel forces believed that destroying urban infrastructure was the most effective way of putting pressure on the government.**

In 1991, there were an estimated 1.25 million head of cattle in El Salvador. Cattle herding has recovered gradually since 1984, when it hit the lowest level of the decade.

AGRICULTURE

El Salvador's wealth was built on the export of just three crops: cacao, indigo, and coffee. This reliance on monocrops could not continue, however, as it made the Salvadoran economy extremely vulnerable to fluctuations in the economies of its trading partners. El Salvador diversified its agricultural exports into cotton, sugar, and, more recently, soya, cucumbers, sesame, tropical flowers, and ornamental plants. Though once a top export, cotton was seriously affected by the civil war and deteriorating economic conditions—many farms were located in the conflict zone and were abandoned—and has virtually disappeared as an export crop. Sugar and shrimp are now the third and fourth largest export commodities. The government has encouraged the development of a shrimp-farming industry in order to prevent overfishing and maintain the shrimp stock.

Coffee is still El Salvador's primary export crop and source of income, generating $151.2 million in earnings in 1992. But the structure of the Salvadoran economy has changed considerably, and agriculture as a whole now accounts for only 10% of the country's gross domestic product. Nevertheless, agriculture is still the backbone of the economy, employing 37% of the labor force, generating approximately 60% of export earnings, and providing about half of the country's food requirements.

COFFEE

Coffee has a long history that is shrouded in legend. First cultivated about A.D. 575, it was not grown extensively until the 15th century. By the 16th and 17th centuries, coffee consumption had spread throughout Persia and Turkey (in the Arab world coffee was dubbed "the wine of Islam"), continental Europe, England, and America. Europeans were in love with the drink—the Viennese developed at least 20 different ways of preparing it. Coffeehouses sprang up everywhere and became popular social, literary, and political gathering places; King Charles II saw them as centers of dissent and tried, unsuccessfully, to shut them down.

Coffee grows wild in Ethiopia, where it originated, but is now cultivated wherever its needs for a hot and moist climate, rich soil, and a high altitude are met. Four of the five billion cultivated coffee trees in the world are found in South America; most of these trees are descendants from just one seedling that was brought to the Caribbean island of Martinique in 1717.

El Salvador has an ideal climate for coffee, but it was not until synthetic dyes made indigo unprofitable in the mid-1800s that El Salvador began to direct its resources toward the large-scale production of coffee beans. This entailed putting the large peasant population to work on the plantations, laying the roads and railroads necessary for transporting the crop, and building processing plants.

Coffee is still El Salvador's primary export crop, but the overproduction of coffee worldwide has led to a drop in prices. In 1993, El Salvador entered into an agreement with the rest of the world's coffee exporters to limit coffee production and thus boost prices.

MANUFACTURING

El Salvador's manufacturing sector experienced rapid growth during the 1960s, but suffered a drastic decline during the 1980s when the civil war caused a shortage of capital and foreign currency, guerrilla sabotage of electrical power plants and factories, protests by labor unions, and reduced demand for products both at home and abroad. Even so, manufacturing has been one of the fastest growing sectors of the economy in recent years and is now the second largest sector of the economy; it totaled 19% of gross domestic product and employed 14% of the work force in 1992. Products such as medicines, soaps, cardboard boxes, synthetic textiles, footwear, and aluminum and copper cables now generate more foreign earnings for El Salvador than do agricultural exports.

Peace has led to a mini-boom in construction.

CONSTRUCTION

Since the 1992 peace accord, the return of capital, private investment, and national reconstruction programs has brought about an annual average growth in the construction industry of about nine percent. Still, construction accounts for a very small part of the overall economy, contributing less than three percent of gross domestic product in 1992.

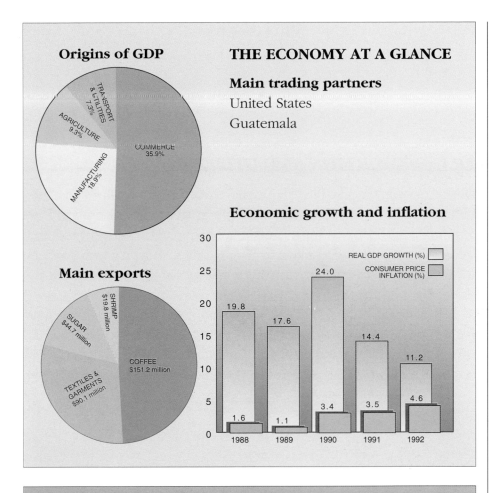

Origins of GDP

TRANSPORT & UTILITIES 7.3%

AGRICULTURE 9.3%

MANUFACTURING 18.9%

COMMERCE 35.9%

Main exports

SUGAR $44.7 million

SHRIMP $19.8 million

TEXTILES & GARMENTS $90.1 million

COFFEE $151.2 million

THE ECONOMY AT A GLANCE

Main trading partners
United States
Guatemala

Economic growth and inflation

REAL GDP GROWTH (%)
CONSUMER PRICE INFLATION (%)

Year	Real GDP Growth (%)	Consumer Price Inflation (%)
1988	1.6	19.8
1989	1.1	17.6
1990	3.4	24.0
1991	3.5	14.4
1992	4.6	11.2

Commerce is by far the most important sector of the economy.

MONEY FROM ABROAD

An estimated one quarter of El Salvador's population currently lives in the United States, and the money they send back home contributes substantially to the country's economy. Foreign aid and the return of private investment capital have also increased since peace was negotiated in 1992. This heavy inflow of foreign funds could soon dry up, however; the United States may force Salvadoran refugees to return home, foreign aid will decrease once postwar reconstruction is complete, and an unfavorable outcome in the 1994 elections could put a stop to private investment.

TRANSPORTATION AND UTILITIES

During the war, much of El Salvador's infrastructure was severely damaged by guerrilla forces. Peace has brought pledges of financial support from around the world for the reconstruction of major highways, power plants, electrical towers, and telecommunications facilities. With only one telephone for every 50 people, there is the potential for significant growth in the telecommunications industry.

El Salvador depends on imported oil for approximately one-third of its energy needs. Since the oil price shocks of 1973 and 1979, when the world supply of petroleum was drastically reduced, El Salvador has tried to decrease its dependence on imported petroleum by developing alternative

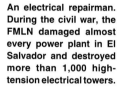

An electrical repairman. During the civil war, the FMLN damaged almost every power plant in El Salvador and destroyed more than 1,000 high-tension electrical towers.

forms of energy. Four hydroelectric plants generate about half of the country's electricity, while the geothermal power station at Ahuachapán contributes another 15%.

LAND REFORM

Land reform has been a thorny issue in El Salvador for over a hundred years. Many attempts to redistribute land from the few large landowners to the majority of landless peasants have ended either in failure or in only partial success, contributing to the country's long history of poverty and violence.

In 1976, President Colonel Molina proposed modest land reform, but he faced violent opposition from the oligarchy who accused him of "turning socialist." The subsequent rise in the murder of peasants by death squads led Colonel Molina to backtrack on his policy.

In 1980, the first of three proposed phases of land reform was implemented. Two hundred large estates were confiscated and handed over to peasant committees representing 150,000 farm workers. Many leaders of these cooperative farms, however, were later killed by soldiers and death squads. Conservative members of the military also blocked the implementation of the second, and crucial, phase of the reform: redistributing middle-size coffee farms.

Land reform was a key condition of the 1992 peace accord. Under the terms of the agreement, 47,500 families (the families of 15,000 members of the military, 7,500 guerrillas, and 25,000 *tenedores*—people who farmed land that was abandoned during the war) were to receive 8.6 acres of land each. A lack of funding, however, has delayed the process. By May 1993, at the beginning of the planting season, little more than half of the land had been distributed.

Land reform is proceeding very slowly. By April 1993, only 9,700 of 47,500 families had received the land promised to them under the 1992 peace accord.

47

SALVADORANS

THE ORIGINAL PEOPLE of what is now El Salvador were a network of Mayan Indian tribes who inhabited the region for thousands of years. Their descendants, the Pipil Indians, lived in the area when the Spanish arrived in the 16th century, but disease, persecution, and intermarriage has led to their gradual elimination.

Today, over 90% of the Salvadoran population is *mestizo* ("mes-TEE-so")—of mixed Indian and Spanish descent. *Ladino* ("lah-DEE-no") is another term that is often used in Latin America; it applies to any person—whether of European, Indian or *mestizo* descent—who has adopted the Spanish language and Spanish-American culture.

The population in El Salvador is thus largely homogenous ethnically and linguistically, but it is sharply divided between rich and poor. Most of the country's wealth lies in the hands of just two percent of the population, while the majority of Salvadorans live below the poverty line, working on plantations, in factories, or in the military for very low wages.

A small percentage have achieved middleclass status by becoming teachers, doctors, civil servants, or business people, or by rising through the ranks of the military.

Opposite: **A young Salvadoran.**

Below: **For a quick nap, truck drivers attach hammocks to the bottom of their trucks.**

49

DESCENDANTS OF THE PIPIL INDIANS

*In the 1800s,
Indians still made
up 60% of the
population; today,
they are just 5% of
the nation.*

Only five percent of Salvadorans are direct descendants of the Pipil Indians who inhabited El Salvador before the arrival of the Spanish. Primarily Pancho and Izalco Indians, they live in a cluster of villages in southwestern El Salvador near the Guatemalan border. Elaborate ceremonial costumes are reserved for special occasions, but some Indian women still wear a version of the traditional *refajo*, or skirt, with plain white or brightly colored blouses. Only a few elders still speak their native Nahua language. Although the government and the Jesuit-run University of Central America attempted to revive the Nahua language in the 1970s, Indians shied away from the effort once the civil war broke out. A long history of persecution at the hands of the government and the oligarchy has resulted in many Indians refusing even to teach Nahua to their children.

A smiling old Indian man in Chalchuapa. Although a few Indians still wear traditional clothes, most have adopted a Western style of dress.

THE OLIGARCHY

Salvadorans of direct European descent make up only three percent of the population, yet this small white minority has—directly or indirectly—controlled the country's power and wealth for almost 500 years. The oligarchy's lifestyle is much the same as that of wealthy people in any other big, modern, cosmopolitan city: they wear designer clothes, drive luxury cars, and vacation abroad. Even within this elite there is a hierarchy: at the top of the pyramid are the families of the "founding fathers"—the original Spanish settlers of El Salvador; next are the descendants of the bankers and financiers who immigrated from various parts of Europe in the 19th and early 20th centuries; at the bottom are the newly rich Palestinians, Lebanese, and Jews who make up the merchant class. The upper class also includes the officer ranks of the military, although the oligarchy and military remain separate entities and tend not to mix socially.

A maid takes the daughter of a wealthy family to a private school in San Salvador.

A poor family of farm hands. Nearly half of the rural population is landless, and very few of those who do own their own land can grow enough food for their families— the soil is too poor and the plots are too small.

Some urban Salvadorans are so destitute that they are forced to make a living—and sometimes their home—on the cities' garbage dumps.

LANDLESS PEASANTS AND URBAN POOR

Whether they live in the city or in the countryside, most *mestizo* and Indian Salvadorans are very poor, malnourished, illiterate, and unemployed. They try to eke out a living by working on plantations, in factories, or in the military. Agricultural work is seasonal, so even farm workers are out of work for part of the year. Thousands of people flock to the cities each year in search of work despite the disheartening fact that urban unemployment is almost 50%; they do whatever they can to get by, living in makeshift huts and selling fruit and vegetables on the streets.

Middleclass teenagers enjoy a day out near the beach.

THE MIDDLE CLASS

Comprising only about eight percent of the population, El Salvador's middle class includes professional and skilled workers, government employees, school teachers, and small landowners.

Although the middle class has tended to encourage land reform and push for an improvement in the standard of living of most Salvadorans, they have had little direct influence in the country's affairs. Many teachers, doctors, and trade unionists were politically active during the war and frequently became the targets of political military harassment and violence.

Refugees in Usulután line up for a simple meal of beans and tortillas. Many less fortunate refugees starved during the war.

REFUGEES

During the war, at least a quarter of El Salvador's population migrated from the countryside to the cities (or vice versa), or fled the country altogether—to the United States, Mexico, and other Central American countries.

Over a million Salvadorans sought refuge in the United States alone, helping to boost El Salvador's economy by sending money home. Many live in the United States illegally, working in temporary, low-paying jobs such as babysitting, gardening, and dog-walking. Very few Salvadorans have been granted political asylum; many U.S. courts were reluctant to accept that Salvadorans were fleeing political violence rather than simply seeking out a better life, as this acknowledgment would have made it very difficult for the United States to justify continuing its financial and military support of the war in El Salvador. It is likely that the United States will force many Salvadoran refugees to return home in the near future.

Approximately 250,000 Salvadorans fled to Mexico, where large refugee camps were established for people escaping violence in Nicaragua, Guatemala, and El Salvador. An estimated 50,000–100,000 Salvadorans went to Honduras, Panama, and Costa Rica.

Several large refugee groups have returned home from neighboring Central American countries and formed new settlements, or "repatriation" communities, on the sites of villages destroyed during the war. As a tribute, several of these communities are christened with the names of priests who were killed in the war.

CIUDAD ROMERO: A REPATRIATION COMMUNITY

Ciudad Romero serves as a shining example of the perseverance and community spirit of Salvadorans in the face of decades of poverty, suffering, and repression.

In May 1980, the townspeople of Nueva Esparta fled their village after being subjected to bombing and persecution. The group of 365 refugees left El Salvador on foot, traveled through Honduras and Nicaragua, and finally settled on the Atlantic Coast of Panama. There they built a new community, which they called Ciudad Romero in honor of the revered Archbishop Oscar Arnulfo Romero who had been assassinated in El Salvador earlier that year.

In Ciudad Romero they built a chapel and a school, and began to cultivate crops of corn, cacao, and rice. Despite their complete isolation from other communities, which meant that they were unable to sell their crops or buy medicine and other necessities, their community continued to grow.

In January 1991, after more than 10 years in Panama, and after a long process of negotiation with the Salvadoran government, the people of Ciudad Romero were allowed to return home to El Salvador. It took a great deal of support from grassroots organizations and the Catholic Church in El Salvador, but eventually the more than 600 refugees established their new settlement in the department of Usulután, in eastern El Salvador. They built a new school, a cooperative store, a new mill for grinding corn, and a communal kitchen where they make tortillas for the entire community. They celebrate Mass in their new community building, where they also hold council meetings. In Ciudad Romero everyone has a say in the future of the town.

LIFESTYLE

SALVADORANS are a very sociable, hardworking, devout, and generous people, despite considerable hardship and adversity. Friends and family are central to daily life, although migration due to unemployment and civil war has broken many families and communities apart. Poverty abounds in El Salvador, and malnutrition is a serious problem, affecting nearly three-quarters of children under the age of five; since most pregnant women are undernourished themselves, many children start life with serious nutritional deficiencies. The lifestyle of the poor, whether in rural areas or in the cities, revolves around providing food and shelter for the family, and there is little time for leisure or education, or money for the modern conveniences that would make life easier. Wealthier Salvadorans, on the other hand, own cars, work in office buildings, shop in malls, and live in modern houses.

The difference in the lifestyle and standard of living between a wealthy urban professional and a poor rural laborer is immense.

Left: **A "traffic clown" brightens up the day by directing traffic in San Salvador.**

Opposite: **As very few Salvadorans own cars, people crowd onto pickup trucks and buses to get around.**

RURAL LIFE

A young mother carries home firewood. Almost 90% of rural houses are without electricity, so cooking is done over a wood or charcoal fire.

Over half of all Salvadorans live in rural areas; the vast majority of them work for large landowners at an hourly wage that cannot pay for adequate food for their families. Houses are small and very basic, transportation is generally by foot or by horse and cart, and long hours are spent getting through the day's work and household chores. At harvest time, the whole family works in the fields. Illiteracy is high, as children leave school at an early age to work or help out at home.

As most houses have no running water or electricity, rural Salvadorans gather wood or charcoal to cook by fire, and burn candles or kerosene lamps for light. Water is usually collected from rivers and streams, even though the surface water is seriously polluted by agricultural and industrial waste. Because of the widespread danger of cholera, most people have developed the practice of disinfecting the water by adding bleach.

THE WORKLOAD OF A RURAL WOMAN

A typical day for a rural woman begins before dawn. The first task is to fetch water, which may be as far as an hour's walk away. When she gets back, she gathers firewood, builds a fire, and makes the day's supply of tortillas. On top of buying food at the daily market, cooking, washing clothes in the river, cleaning the house, and caring for the children, her tasks include tending the garden and raising chickens and pigs. During the harvest season, she works on the farm alongside her husband, often without pay. She might also try to earn extra money for the family by selling vegetables, homemade fruit drinks, or candles in the local market or at a roadside stand.

Most Salvadoran women wash clothes in the river or lake because they do not have running water at home.

LIFE IN THE CITY

Over one quarter of El Salvador's population lives in the capital city of San Salvador. The downtown streets are congested with cars, buses, street vendors, and pedestrians, and the air is thick with pollution. Most urban Salvadorans work in factories, offices, and shops or as domestic workers. They shop at large central markets or modern, multistory shopping centers. The wide disparity between rich and poor is especially evident in San Salvador. The wealthy live in quiet, elegant suburbs, socialize in private clubs, dine in fine restaurants, and shop in expensive boutiques, while the poor live in slums on the edge of the city, eking out a living as best they can.

HOUSING

Modern San Salvador.

RURAL The most common kind of house, the *choza* ("CHO-sah"), is made of woven branches and covered with mud; others are made of adobe, or sun-dried mud bricks, which are sometimes whitewashed. Houses have dirt floors and thatched or tiled roofs; very few have running water or electricity. Living quarters are typically very crowded, with six or more people living in one or two rooms that are divided by curtains rather than walls. Family members pull out cots, hammocks, or straw mats to sleep on at night.

URBAN The wealthy live in modern houses with swimming pools, well-tended gardens, and elaborate security systems. The small middleclass population lives in row houses or in comfortable apartments, either inside the city or in suburbs. Most of the poor live in *tugurios* ("tu-GU-ryos"), shantytowns made of tin or cardboard, with dirt floors, no electricity, and no access to running water or sewage services, while others rent rooms in crowded, rundown buildings called *mesones* ("may-SON-ays")—chains of tiny, often windowless rooms surrounding a common courtyard, with a common latrine but no washing or cooking facilities.

Salvadorans flock to the capital city of San Salvador in search of work and a better way of life, but over 70% of the people end up living in shantytowns such as this one.

61

Collecting water from a well. Less than 60% of Salvadorans have access to safe drinking water and adequate sanitation.

HEALTH CARE

Health care is a problem for the majority of Salvadorans. Medical facilities are inadequate, especially in rural areas; most of the few hospitals that exist are overcrowded, rundown and badly equipped, and facilities are often insanitary. Patients who go into the hospital for treatment are usually advised to bring their own bedsheets, food, soap, toilet paper, and even surgical supplies.

Qualified doctors and nurses are in short supply. In 1989, the Ministry of Planning in El Salvador reported that there were only 12 hospital beds, 3.2 doctors, and 2.1 nurses for every 10,000 people.

The shortage of medical facilities often means that only patients needing emergency surgery receive treatment, while non-urgent cases are forced to wait. At the Rosales Hospital in 1990, an estimated 20,000 people were on the waiting list for elective surgery.

Poor sanitation and a lack of access to safe drinking water, especially among rural dwellers, cause a high number of deaths from waterborne diseases such as diarrhea and enteritis. Malnutrition, resulting from an inadequate consumption of calories and protein, is another leading cause of death in both adults and children. In 1990, the average daily consumption of protein was only 55.2 grams, compared to 111.1 grams in the United States. The 12-year civil war only made it harder for Salvadorans to find adequate and nutritious food for themselves and their families.

Adult life expectancy, however, has improved in El Salvador over the past decade. In 1985, the average male life expectancy was 50.7 years, while average female life expectancy was 63.9. Five years later, average life expectancy had increased to 58.1 years for men and 66.9 for women. Nevertheless, these figures still lag far behind those of the United States, where the average male baby born in 1990 could expect to live until the age of 71.6, and the average female baby until the age of 78.5.

Almost two-thirds of the population have no access to medical care.

A HARSH LIFE

Exiled Salvadoran novelist Manlio Argueta describes her life in El Salvador in her book *One Day In Life*. Her parents could send her only to the first grade because there were too many children. There were 14 in the family, including 11 brothers. There would have been 17, but 3 children had died of dehydration before their first birthday. She remembers how her father held the last child to die by his feet, believing that if blood ran to his head, he would be saved.

Since she was the only girl in the family, Manlio was put in charge of grinding corn and cooking it and then taking it to her brothers in the cornfields. She and her mother took care of the house.

THE FAMILY

The family is central to life in El Salvador, and families tend to be large, partly due to the dominance of Roman Catholicism, and partly through necessity. In rural areas, especially, women are urged to marry young and have several children; children are considered an economic asset and are relied upon to help earn income for the family and to care for their parents in their old age.

One-third of rural women become pregnant by the age of 14, and the average rural woman gives birth nine times. The high birth rate is a way of compensating for the high infant mortality rate—many rural children die in their first year from disease or malnutrition. In cities, the birth rate is lower, with the average urban woman giving birth to five children.

The two-child family is a rarity in El Salvador. The average rural woman gives birth 8 to 10 times, although only half the children will survive past the age of one.

Women head many
Salvadoran families.

Family unity is important, and extended families are common, with three generations often living under the same roof. Upper-class families are tied to one another by a complex web of marriage and kinship; this is one of the ways in which they have managed to hold on to their power and wealth.

The influence of Catholicism has broadened the concept of family to include *padrinos* ("pa-DREE-nos," or godfathers) and *madrinas* ("ma-DREE-nas," or godmothers). Godparents are expected to play an important role in a child's upbringing.

Family support has helped poor people endure the years of poverty and hardship, although civil war and chronic unemployment have taken their toll on family unity in rural areas. Although Salvadoran society is traditionally patriarchal, as is the case in most of Latin America, many rural families are in fact headed by women, as the men left home in search of work or to fight in the war. Common-law marriages are increasingly common in rural areas.

Many women joined the guerrilla forces during the war. Men and women were treated as equals— women shared in the fighting and men shared in the cooking.

THE POSITION OF WOMEN

Women in El Salvador have faced widespread exploitation and oppression due to the circumstances of poverty, war, or simply tradition. Domestic abuse by fathers and husbands is not uncommon, and women working as maids are often sexually abused by their employers. *Machismo*, the Latin American ideal of manliness, dictates that men are superior to women, that a husband should earn the money for his family, and that the wife should do the "women's work" of cooking, cleaning, and caring for the children. The economic reality in El Salvador, however, is that most families require two income-earning parents. The social reality is that many men abandon their wives, leaving about one quarter of all households headed by women.

Guerrilla groups tried to overcome the widespread attitude of women as inferior beings. In the areas they controlled during the war, they discouraged wife-beating and stressed the equality of women in almost every aspect of work. Men and women shared responsibility for cooking, washing clothes, and working on construction and development projects.

Many Salvadoran women themselves have started to act as a force for positive change, forming organizations to tackle some of the fundamental issues that have prevented women from achieving equality, especially in rural areas: the lack of education, the high infant mortality rate, and the high birth rate. These organizations provide a broad range of medical, legal, child care, family planning, job placement, and educational services.

Women have made progress in professional fields; 30% of El Salvador's physicians and lawyers, and almost 50% of the country's dentists and high school teachers are women. The government has passed laws granting women equal legal status and "equal pay for equal work," but in practice many women still face discrimination in the workplace.

Landowners often refuse to pay women for their labor.

EDUCATION

El Salvador's commitment to education and even basic literacy has been seriously hindered by the war and compromised by poverty. Although 73% of the adult population is literate, literacy rates vary considerably with age. Nearly half of Salvadorans over the age of 65, for example, are illiterate.

The education system is structured so that children are required to attend one year of preschool, nine years of basic education, and finally three years of secondary education (the equivalent of high school in the

School under the trees. Less than two-thirds of rural children attend primary school, and only 20% complete the sixth grade.

United States). Students then have the option of continuing their education at the military academy or at one of El Salvador's two universities or nine technological institutions.

In reality, a small minority of students complete 12 years of schooling; only 7% of school-age Salvadorans enter high school, and nearly one-third of Salvadorans over the age of 10 have no schooling whatsoever. Tuition is free, but even the cost of supplies is too expensive for many poor families. This problem is compounded by a shortage of teachers and schools, and the need for many children to leave school after only a year or two, in order to help support their family.

Very few Salvadorans—about 2% of the population, compared to about 32% in the United States—attend college or university. The University of Central America, a private university in San Salvador run by Jesuit priests and dubbed "the Princeton of Central America," attracts mainly upper-class Salvadorans. Poorer students tend to go to the National University. In 1989, only 1,459 students graduated with a degree. Most of these graduates were in the fields of teaching and law.

A statue at a San Salvador university is riddled by bullets. Campuses were hotbeds of activism during the civil war and prime targets of military crackdowns.

Highways are used mainly by trucks and buses, while most Salvadorans get around on mules, horses, bicycles, and on foot.

TRANSPORTATION

El Salvador has almost 10,000 miles of roads as well as two major highways (the Pan American Highway and the Carretora Litoral) that run the length of the country. These roads, however, are more likely to be traveled by buses and trucks than by private cars, as less than two percent of the population own a car.

Taxis are plentiful in the capital city of San Salvador, but most Salvadorans get around by bus, bicycle, or on foot. In rural areas and in Indian villages, horses are another common form of transportation. The bus system is extensive and is the most popular method of traveling long distances.

Trains and boats are rarely used. Ferrocarriles Nacionales de El Salvador, the national railway, is responsible for several hundred miles of railroad, but has failed to keep it in good condition; slow and inefficient, the railway is used mainly for transporting goods. Similarly, El Salvador's two main ports have declined in recent years.

By contrast, the international airport near San Salvador is one of the most modern in the region and is served by a number of international airlines. Transportes Aéreos Centroamericanos (TACA), El Salvador's privately owned national airline, is Central America's largest air carrier and flies passengers to all Central American capital cities, Mexico City, and most major U.S. cities.

SHOPPING

In San Salvador, the most popular shopping places are the central market, which covers an entire city block, and Metrocentro, a modern, split-level shopping mall offering a wide variety of goods in air-conditioned boutiques. In smaller towns and villages, open-air markets and general stores stock a limited range of basic goods such as clothing, food and household goods.

EATING OUT

Dining out in one of San Salvador's many upscale restaurants is a luxury that few ordinary Salvadorans can afford, but there are many popular alternatives offering a quick and inexpensive bite to eat. *Pupuserías* ("poo-poo-say-REE-as"), sidewalk vendors, and market kitchens sell a variety of local specialties. American fast-food chain restaurants can also be found in San Salvador.

Below: **A boutique in San Salvador's Metrocentro shopping mall sells imported clothing.**

Bottom: **Small restaurants like this one abound in El Salvador. Most serve stuffed tortillas, a Salvadoran specialty that is very time-consuming to make at home.**

RELIGION

THE STRONGEST RELIGIONS in El Salvador today are Catholicism, evangelical Protestantism, and liberation theology. Like much of Latin America, El Salvador is an intensely religious society—even non-practicing Catholics and people not affiliated with any religion say they pray at least once a day.

Roman Catholicism was brought to Latin America as part of the Spanish Conquest, and it has played an extremely important role in shaping the culture of the region. In El Salvador, the Catholic Church generally supported the ruling classes and the social and economic systems that caused much hardship for the majority of Salvadorans. Even so, over 80% of Salvadorans are Catholic. Church rituals and symbols have permeated society, and Catholicism's traditions of community, hierarchy, and social ties remain strong.

In recent years, there has been an increase in the popularity of liberation theologists, Baha'is, and Protestant sects such as Evangelical Christians, Mormons, Seventh Day Adventists, and Jehovah's Witnesses—all of which are gradually eroding the dominance of Roman Catholicism. Evangelical church services provide a supportive and charismatic environment that is particularly appealing to large numbers of Salvadorans who are poor and displaced from their community.

Opposite: **A nun gives advice to a peasant outside the cathedral in San Salvador.**

Above: **A simple cross marks the grave of a Salvadoran peasant.**

73

CATHOLICISM

The dominance of Catholicism in El Salvador is clear by the number of religious holidays and festivals that fill the Salvadoran calendar and the abundance of Catholic churches, symbols, and shrines throughout the country. Every town and every Catholic church in El Salvador has a patron saint who is feted every year with great pomp and festivity.

Despite its widespread popularity, Catholicism is beginning to lose its grip on many aspects of life. Both civil and religious marriage ceremonies are less prevalent in El Salvador than in other Latin American countries, and there is a relatively high rate of family breakdown. Divorces and common-law marriages are on the rise, and many children are born out of wedlock. Also, the practice of selecting godparents for children is becoming less widespread.

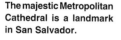

The majestic Metropolitan Cathedral is a landmark in San Salvador.

CATHOLIC SHRINES

Catholic shrines in El Salvador attract pilgrims and visitors from far and wide. The Virgin Mary is a particularly important symbol, as it is in every Catholic society, and several outdoor shrines have been erected in her honor.

An elegant white shrine, La Ceiba de Guadalupe, stands in San Salvador in tribute to the Vírgen de Guadalupe. December 12 is her celebration day.

The small town of Cojutepeque, near San Salvador, attracts a steady flow of pilgrims, especially on May 13. There, in a large park on the Hill of the Turkeys, is the shrine of the Vírgen de Fátima, who is said to have appeared to three Portuguese shepherd children on May 13, 1917. The statue was brought to El Salvador from Fátima, Portugal, in 1949.

This breakdown of the family is due partly to widespread poverty but also to the strain caused by war and migratory work patterns. The Catholic Church is trying to reverse these trends by borrowing an idea from the liberation theologists' Christian base communities and the increasingly popular evangelical and Protestant groups. The Church hierarchy has initiated a social program called the "new evangelization of the laity;" parish priests are attempting to develop a "new culture" by emphasizing the need for small, closely-knit communities that provide a sense of belonging to their members.

THE INFLUENCE OF CATHOLICISM

As is the practice in other predominantly Catholic countries, public holidays in El Salvador center on religious events such as Christmas and Easter, and every town has a festival for its patron saint. Salvadorans attach a lot of importance to the rites of passage, celebrating them with a great deal of religious symbolism. Babies are formally christened and baptized into the church; *padrinos* ("pa-DREE-nos"), or godparents, are carefully chosen for each child and are given the responsibility of guiding the child's spiritual—and sometimes material—development; entrance into adulthood during the child's 15th year is celebrated with a church ceremony called a *quinciñera* ("keen-see-NYE-rah"); weddings are always formal occasions and usually take place in a church; death is "celebrated" with a *vela* ("VAY-lah"), or wake. The degree of luxury at the festivities surrounding all these ceremonies depends on the wealth of the family, but they are always treated as important, joyous events, celebrated with an abundance of food, drink, music, and dancing.

THE RISE OF LIBERATION THEOLOGY

In the late 1960s, some members of the Roman Catholic Church began to talk about the need to "give the Church back to the people." This meant saying Mass in Spanish instead of Latin and applying the Bible to contemporary problems. Priests and lay leaders began to work with the poor and try to improve their quality of life physically as well as spiritually. People formed small groups called "Christian base communities," which discussed how situations described in the Bible could be applied to their own lives, and started agitating for change. As a result of this challenge to the existing social and political order, many members of the oligarchy and the military began to view the Church as subversive and Communist. Several church workers and members of Christian base communities became targets of violence.

Violence continued throughout the 1980s, causing so many priests to resign that nearly half of the rural parishes were left without one. Many of the Christian base communities dissolved or went underground, continuing their activities in secret. Many lay leaders of the Christian base communities joined the guerrillas, and some priests continued working in the conflict zones, trying to emphasize the need for social and political organization among the poor. Many were assassinated. The violence against Archbishop Oscar Arnulfo Romero and other popular priests turned them into martyrs and added fire to the cause. The new archbishop, Monsignor Arturo Rivera y Damás, distanced himself and the Church hierarchy from the growing political struggle. Still, liberation theology continued to have its mobilizing effect at the grassroots level.

Over the years, a "people's church" has emerged that has acted more or less independently of the Catholic hierarchy and has succeeded in attracting many Salvadorans away from Roman Catholicism.

Liberation theology challenged the Catholic Church's traditional stance of teaching people to overlook their misfortunes on earth and to wait for their reward in heaven; instead, it encouraged people to take an active role in bettering their own lives.

ARCHBISHOP ROMERO

Faced with the rise of liberation theology and a challenge to the status quo, in 1977 the Vatican appointed Monsignor Oscar Arnulfo Romero to be the new archbishop and to reinforce a conservative authority in El Salvador. As Archbishop Romero became familiar

with the reality of life in El Salvador, however, he began to speak out against the widespread repression and poverty he saw. He encouraged workers to campaign for an increase in wages and a redistribution of land, and called on the govern-ment to end repression and bring about social justice.

Within two years, the small, soft-spoken and bespectacled Archbishop Romero had become a much-loved figure among the ordinary people of El Salvador. But he was viewed as a major threat by the government and the military. Branded as a guerrilla, he was assassinated while celebrating Mass on March 24, 1980. The murder shocked people both inside and outside El Salvador and was one of the events that sparked the outbreak of civil war.

Although the government officially attributed the murder to unidentified members of rightwing death squads, Roberto d'Aubuisson, leader of the ARENA party, was widely believed to be responsible. At the end of the civil war 12 years later, the Truth Commission, mandated by the peace agreement to investigate the worst crimes of the war, found that Roberto d'Aubuisson had indeed ordered the murder of Archbishop Romero.

Archbishop Romero is believed to have made a radical shift away from conservatism after the assassination of his good friend Father Rutilio Grande. Father Rutilio was a Jesuit priest who believed in liberation theology and was outspoken in defense of the poor. When he was killed, Archbishop Romero felt he could no longer ignore the brutality of the government.

PROTESTANTS

Protestantism has enjoyed a tremendous growth and has contributed to the decline of the Catholic Church in El Salvador, although only about 12% of Salvadorans are Protestants. Evangelical missionaries, primarily from the United States, have become so influential that all non-Catholic groups working and preaching in Central America, including Presbyterians, Lutherans, Mormons, and Jehovah's Witnesses, are referred to as "evangelicals."

Although evangelicals use some of the same techniques as liberation theologists, meeting in small groups and emphasizing prayer and personal responsibility, they generally discourage efforts to achieve social and political change and have thus won the support of the oligarchy and the military. On the other hand, some of the more mainstream Protestant groups, such as Baptists, Episcopalians, and Lutherans, espoused liberation theology and won many converts among the poor.

Protestants in El Salvador tend to be less educated, work in lower-status occupations, and earn less money than most Catholics.

Inside an evangelical church. Evangelicals tend to be especially fervent in their worship, and attend church twice as often as Catholics do.

INDIAN RELIGION

The religion practiced by Indians in Central America has been described by anthropologists as Christo-pagan due to its complex mix of indigenous beliefs and the Christianity of early Roman Catholic missionaries.

Christian baptism, for example, is the first major event in the life of an individual, and a child is not considered fully human until the baptism has been performed. At the other end of the life cycle, the usual Christian rituals are observed: at funerals, the body is buried, church bells are rung, incense is burned, and prayers are read in church and at the graveside. Christian deities and saints have replaced the hierarchy of indigenous supernatural beings, but pagan beliefs remain: for example, disease is attributed to witchcraft or the failure to appease evil spirits.

A church in the Indian village of Panchimalco reflects the typical blend of indigenous and Christian influences.

THE INDIAN STORY OF CREATION

Indians in Central America believed that four worlds or "Suns" were created by gods and then destroyed by catastrophes before the present universe came into being.

According to the Aztec legend of creation, the first Sun was called "Four-Jaguar" and was destroyed by jaguars; at the end of the second Sun, "Four-Wind," mankind was transformed into monkeys by a hurricane unleashed by the wind god; the god of thunder and lightning put an end to the third Sun, "Four-Rain," with a rain of fire; and the fourth Sun, "Four-Water," ended in a massive flood that lasted for 52 years. The fifth and present Sun, "Four-Earthquake," was created by the rain god and is doomed to be destroyed by a tremendous earthquake.

The Aztecs believed that their mission was to prevent the fifth destruction of the Earth, and that the only way of doing this was to appease the sun with offerings and sacrifices.

FOLK BELIEFS

Belief in the power of witchcraft and the devil is widespread, and good and evil spirits are prominent figures in folktales. *Brujería* ("brew-hay-REE-ya"), or witchcraft, is really a form of Indian medicine practiced in some rural areas. The *curandero* ("cur-ahn-DE-roh"), or witch doctor, is believed to have special healing powers and uses herbs and other

This Indian medicine shop offers traditional herbal remedies for a variety of illnesses.

traditional medicines to treat illnesses that do not respond to conventional Western medicine. For example, people from the city travel to Indian villages to ask *curanderos* for special powders and rituals that they hope will improve their love life.

A traditional remedy for a sick baby involves the *curandero* rubbing garlic paste on the baby's body, hanging a ring of garlic around the baby's neck, praying, and holding an egg up to the sun; if the *curandero* can see a small circle in the white part of the egg, it means that someone has looked at the baby with "sight that is too strong," and the treatment of garlic paste and prayer is continued.

LANGUAGE

WHILE INDIAN LANGUAGES have continued to flourish in some Central and South American countries—Mayan in Guatemala, Quechua in Peru, and Guaraní in Paraguay, for example—the indigenous languages of El Salvador have died out in daily use. Nahua and Lenca, derived from the Nahuatl language of the Aztecs, began to decline when Spain colonized El Salvador in the 16th century and most Indians became assimilated into Spanish-American culture. The massacre of 30,000 Indians in 1932 further eroded the position of indigenous languages; it was a turning point in Salvadoran history when most of the country's remaining Indians were forced to abandon their native languages, customs, and costumes in order to survive. Spanish is now the official language of El Salvador and is spoken by the vast majority of its citizens.

Left: **Spanish dominates almost every aspect of Salvadoran life; all shop signs and street signs are in Spanish.**

Opposite: **Despite widespread illiteracy, Salvadorans have a choice of five daily newspapers.**

INDIGENOUS LANGUAGES

Pipil, a Nahua language, and Chilanga, a Lenca language, are almost extinct in El Salvador, spoken by fewer than 2,000 Indians. The most obvious legacy of these languages exists in the country's geographical names. Cuscatlán, the Nahua name for the area that includes present-day El Salvador, means "Land of the Jewel." Towns and villages such as Chalchuapa, Nahuizalco and Zacatecoluca all bear names of Pipil origin. Many of the natural landmarks also retain their indigenous names, such as the Izalco Volcano, the Lempa River, and Lake Coatepeque. Most of the volcanoes have both an Indian name and a Spanish name: the San Salvador Volcano, for instance, is also known as Quetzaltepec, meaning "mountain of quetzal birds" in Nahua.

SPANISH

The phenomenon of military rule in El Salvador and throughout Latin America has spawned words such as junta *and* generalissimo *that are understood everywhere.*

The Spanish spoken in El Salvador and other Central and South American countries is close to that of Spain, although there are some variations in local vocabulary and expressions. A soft drink, for example, is called a *gaseosa* ("ga-say-OH-sah") in El Salvador and Honduras, a *soda* ("SOH-dah") in Panama, and a *fresco* ("FRAY-skoh") in Nicaragua. One feature common to the pronunciation in all of Spanish America is the tendency to make "s," "z," and soft "c" into the same sound "s."

Although Spanish has replaced the indigenous languages in El Salvador, it has also been influenced by them. When the colonialists came across new types of food and animals, they used an approximation of the native Indian names to create new words: thus *maíz* ("may-EES," corn), *cacao* ("ka-KAY-oh," cocoa) and *ananás* ("ah-nah-NAHS," pineapple), as well as tapir, jaguar, and llama.

SPANISH: LANGUAGE OF THE CONQUISTADORES

In the 10th century, at the height of the Arabic civilization, the survival of Spanish in the world seemed unlikely. A few hundred years later, however, Spanish had become a major colonizing language, and today, Spanish is spoken by six times as many people outside than inside Spain.

Spanish gained its first foothold in the Americas when the explorer Hernán Cortés landed in 1519 and overthrew Montezuma's Aztec empire. As the Spanish conquistadores spread across the continent in search of gold, they brought their language with them. Spanish is now the official language of all mainland countries in Central and South America, with the exception of Brazil, Belize, and the Guyanas. From Mexico to the tip of Argentina, Spanish is spoken by more than 300 million people.

With the population of the region expected to increase rapidly by the end of the century, Spanish is assured of an even greater prominence among the world's languages.

Salvadoran
Spanish includes
animal references.
For example, when
Salvadorans sit
down after a long
day and sigh, "Me
duelan mis patas,"
they are voicing
the equivalent of
"My dogs (feet) are
killing me." Patas
literally means
paws.Salvadorans
also refer to their
children as
patojos, which is a
derivative of pato,
or duck.

SALVADORAN PRONUNCIATION

Unlike Spanish speakers in some Latin American countries, Salvadorans typically speak clearly and precisely, pronouncing every syllable of every word.

a	*a* as in cart
e	*e* as in they or *a* as in day
i	*ee* as in meet
o	*o* as in note
u	*oo* as in toot or *u* as in flute
y	*ee* as in meet or *y* as in yet
b	*b* as in boy
c	*s* as in sit when before *e* or *i*, or *k* as in kind
ch	*ch* as in child
d	*d* as in dog; or resembles *th* as in they when at the end of a word
f	*f* as in off
g	*g* as in go, or, when before *e* or *i*, a guttural *ch* as in loch
h	silent
j	*h* as in hat
l	*l* as in ball
ll	*y* as in yet
m	*m* as in map
n	*n* as in noon
ñ	*ny* as in canyon
p	*p* as in purse
q	*k* as in kind
r	rolled, especially when at the beginning of a word
rr	strongly rolled
s	*s* as in sit
t	*t* as in tilt
v	*b* as in boy
x	*x* as in exit
z	*s* as in sit

NAMES AND TITLES

Many Salvadorans follow the Spanish custom of having two or more surnames, taking the patrimonial surname from both parents to form the surname. For instance, Liliana Guadalupe Escobar Hernandez officially has four names: the first two are hers alone; the third name, Escobar, is her father's surname, which was also his father's family name; the fourth name, Hernandez, is her mother's family name. Formally, Liliana is known as Señorita Escobar Hernandez, often shortened to Señorita Escobar. If she marries a man named Oscar Hurtado Gomez, she will take the patrilineal part of his surname and add it to hers: Liliana Guadalupe Escobar Hurtado. Then she will formally be called Señora Hurtado.

NONVERBAL COMMUNICATION

Nonverbal forms of communication provide important clues to a country's culture and people. As in most Hispanic cultures, Salvadorans greet each other and say goodbye with a single kiss on the cheek. Between men and women, and among women, a single meeting is enough of a basis to salute each other with a kiss. Men exchange handshakes with their male acquaintances and hugs with close male friends.

THE MEDIA

It's not surprising that basic forms of communication tend to prevail in a society characterized by widespread illiteracy, poverty, and a lack of electricity. Thus battery-operated radios are more widespread than television sets, storytelling is a more popular form of entertainment than reading books, and radio and word of mouth are more common than newspapers as sources of news. The clandestine radio station Radio Venceremos played a crucial role during the war, providing guerrillas and civilians with news of the war and details of the army's activities.

Radio plays an important role in educating adult Salvadorans.

NEWSPAPERS

Despite the high illiteracy rate, Salvadorans have a wide choice of newspapers. *La Prensa*, *El Diario de Hoy*, and *La Noticia* are published every morning, while *El Mundo* and *Diario Latino* appear in the afternoon. In 1990, the dailies had a total circulation of 457,000—or one newspaper for every 12 Salvadorans. As in many Latin American countries where the press is subjected to censorship, most papers tell the news from the government's point of view. Although *La Prensa* is said to provide the best coverage of day-to-day news events, *Diario Latino* has the reputation of being the most objective.

ARTS

EL SALVADOR'S most notable developments in the areas of literature, music, and painting have occurred in the last 200 years. It was only after independence that national arts institutions were established, spawning the first music conservatory, a symphony orchestra, and an academy of art.

Given El Salvador's turbulent past, it is not surprising that much of the country's artistic expression has been influenced by politics. Paintings, plays, books, and music typically contain elements that are political in nature. At least three of the best-known Salvadoran writers have been forced to flee government repression for their political activities, and they live in exile abroad.

El Salvador also has a strong tradition of popular art in the form of folk music, popular theater, and folk art. Elements of indigenous art have recently begun to influence Salvadoran music and painting.

Opposite: **A ceramic vessel made by the Mayan Indians.**

Below: **This mural shows a typical Salvadoran scene of a family working on a coffee plantation.**

The life-size statue of an ancient priest wearing the skin of a sacrificial victim inside-out is displayed at the national museum.

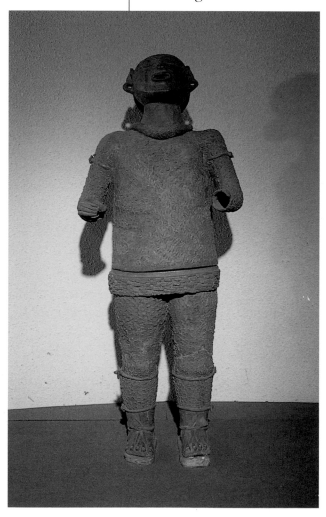

ANCIENT ARTS AND CRAFTS

Most of what is known of Mayan and Aztec art forms is drawn from archeological discoveries of ancient artifacts. Musical instruments include pipes with as many as six finger holes; drums, called *huehuetls* ("hway-HWAY-tls"), made from wood or clay and originally covered with deerskin; and marimbas, or wooden xylophones, which were introduced to the Pipil Indians from Mexico and Guatemala; the *pito* ("PEE-toh"), a high-pitched whistle that sounds like a flute; and the *chirmía* ("cheer-MEE-ah"), which is a pipe with a reed mouthpiece that sounds rather like a clarinet. Percussion instruments include the *tambor* ("tam-BOHR"), a large drum, and the *tun* ("TOON"), a small drum.

Musical instruments, pottery vessels, stone sculptures, and jewelry made from copper, gold, and jade attest to the magnificence of the crafts produced by Indians thousands of years ago.

Many of the artifacts unearthed at the ruins of ancient cities in El Salvador are now housed in the Museo Nacional Davíd J. Guzmán—the national museum in San Salvador—and at the Tazumal museum.

PAINTING

It was not until the 20th century that El Salvador produced notable painters. The most famous contemporary Salvadoran painter is José Mejía Vides, who is sometimes called the "Painter of Panchimalco" because he often portrays small-town life in his paintings. His vivid, simple style shows the influence of Mexico's famous muralists and of the French painter Paul Gauguin.

Julia Díaz is El Salvador's best-known female painter. She studied in Paris, and her work has been exhibited in the United States, Europe, and Latin America. Other contemporary painters include Raúl Elias Reyes, Luis Angel Salinas, Camilio Minero, and Noé Canjura, all of whom have shown their work internationally. Canjura sold his painting "Indian Christ" to the government of Guatemala.

A notable and unique school of art has recently been founded by Salvadoran painter Fernando Llort in the town of La Palma. La Palma art uses bright colors and a naive style to portray religious themes as well as the peasants, the farm animals, and the red-roofed white adobe houses of rural El Salvador. The images are painted onto wooden crosses, cast into ceramics, or finely etched on seeds to be worn as pendants.

Fernando Llort has also produced many excellent sculptures and canvas paintings, which he displays in his own gallery, El Arbol de Dios, in San Salvador.

A shopkeeper uses art to attract customers and advertise his wares.

Right: A craftsman in Ilobasco paints ceramic figures.

Below: Hammocks and other colorful woven textiles have been hand-made in the village of San Sebastián for well over a hundred years.

HANDICRAFTS

Since the time of the Maya many thousands of years ago, crafts have played a prominent role among the Indians of Central America. Musical instruments, pottery vessels, stone sculptures, architectural ornaments, and jewelry found at the sites of ruined cities offer proof of the level of skill attained by Mayan craftsmen. In some areas, entire communities specialized in a particular craft. Craftsmen were organized into guilds and enjoyed considerable prestige in society.

Several Indian villages near San Salvador continue to specialize in traditional handicrafts. Ilobasco, one of the country's foremost traditional craft villages, is famous for its intricate ceramics and *sorpresas* ("sorh-PRAY-sas"), or "surprises," which are tiny clay figures and nativity scenes hidden inside walnut-sized oval shells. Basketry is the specialty of Nahuizalco, a Pipil Indian village. Colorful hammocks and other woven textiles made on handmade wooden looms form the basis of San Sebastián's economy.

LITERATURE

Poetry has a strong tradition in El Salvador and is extremely popular among people from all walks of life. The 19th century poet Juan José Cañas Gavidia spent most of his life living abroad and writing nostalgically about El Salvador's lakes and volcanoes. Poet, essayist, playwright, translator, historian, and dramatist Francisco Antonio Gavidia died in 1955 at the age of 90. His most important poem, "To Central America," condemned tyranny and expressed faith in democracy and the unity of Central America.

Salvador Salazar Arrué, who wrote under the pen name Salarrué, was a novelist, short story writer, and painter. His short story, *Cuentos de Barro*, or "Tales of Mud," is said to mark the beginning of the modern Central American short story genre.

Two of the best—and most controversial—writers of the 20th century are Roque Dalton and Manlio Argueta. Roque Dalton was a poet and historian who was born into a wealthy family but spoke out against El Salvador's social injustices. He was arrested by government forces and sentenced to be executed, but he escaped and went into exile from 1960 to 1973. When he returned to El Salvador, he joined the guerrilla army but was charged with spying; he was tried and executed by guerrillas in 1975. His collection of poetry, *Clandestine Poems*, was translated into English in 1986.

Manlio Argueta writes about the daily life and struggles of the Salvadoran peasants. He was expelled from El Salvador four times because of his political activism and is currently living in exile in Costa Rica. His books, *One Day of Life* and *Cuzcatlán*, have been translated into English.

Claribel Alegría has authored more than 15 books, translated into 11 languages. She lives in exile in Spain.

A tribute to Roque Dalton, a prominent Salvadoran writer who was exiled by government forces in 1960 and executed by the guerrilla army in 1975.

MUSIC

Formal music performances are held at San Salvador's National Theater. David Granadino and Felipe Soto are two renowned 19th century composers whose music is still performed today. One of El Salvador's most famous 20th century composers is María Mendoza de Baratta, who is greatly influenced by indigenous Salvadoran music.

Canción popular ("kan-see-OHN poh-poo-LAHR"), or folk music, which describes daily life and current events in El Salvador, is performed in bars, cafés, at music festivals, and at an open forum called a *peña* ("PAY-nya"), where anyone from the audience can stand up and play or sing. Andean folk music, the distinctive Incan music of the Andes played on pan pipes and flutes, is also popular in El Salvador.

THEATER

Formal theater performances are held at the ornate National Theater in San Salvador. Contemporary dramatists include Waldo Chávez Velasco, who writes fantasy, and Italo López Vallecillos and Alvaro Menén Desleal, both distinguished popular authors of political and philosophical works.

Popular theater, on the other hand, is usually performed in cafés and at outdoor festivals, and often draws from political subject matter. During the civil war, this type of theater was often performed with a certain degree of risk, because it usually carried a message of protest against the government, and the military often responded with harassment and violence against the performers.

POLITICAL ART

Political murals and graffiti adorn many university campus buildings, banners, and walls throughout the city of San Salvador. Salvadorans have used this popular art form to express their feelings and frustrations about various aspects of the 12-year civil war. The "Mothers of the Disappeared" mounted photographs and paintings of their loved ones  onto banners when staging their demonstrations. Students sprayed anti-U.S. slogans and drawings of Uncle Sam and American troops onto walls; and leftwing supporters wrote protests against government violence in huge letters on the city's sidewalks.

LEISURE

DAILY LIFE is hard work in El Salvador, especially in rural areas; with the whole family toiling long hours just to get by, there is little time left for play and little or no money for toys or hobbies. Salvadoran children still play when they can, of course, making "toys" from sticks, tin cans, stones, or rags, and playing *mica* ("MEE-ka"), or tag. Soccer is extremely popular, and those who cannot afford to buy a proper football make do with a nylon stocking wrapped around a ball of rags. After the evening meal, friends and neighbors often gather together—the women to talk, the men to drink and gamble. Wealthier Salvadorans living in the capital have more sophisticated leisure choices: they can dine in fine restaurants, see plays at the National Theater, dance in nightclubs, or listen to concerts performed by El Salvador's symphony orchestra.

Opposite: **A child at play.**

Left: **Market stall workers take a break from the heat of the midday sun.**

SPORTS

Volleyball, basketball, baseball, and softball are popular in El Salvador, but *fútbol,* or soccer, is the country's national sport. Its fans are passionate in their enjoyment of the game, whether they are playing it themselves or just watching it. Almost every city has a soccer stadium, and young boys join neighborhood or school teams at an early age, hoping to be chosen one day to play for the *Selección Nacional,* the national team.

Water sports are also popular in El Salvador, especially during the hottest months. Wealthier Salvadorans enjoy swimming at private clubs or beaches, water-skiing, boating, and fishing, while poor rural children are happy simply to splash about in lakes or rivers while their mothers wash clothes. One of the most popular spots for swimming is Los Chorros, a beautiful park near San Salvador.

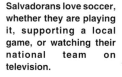

Salvadorans love soccer, whether they are playing it, supporting a local game, or watching their national team on television.

THE SOCCER WAR

Unfortunately, politics can intrude into the realm of sports, as it did in the "soccer war" of 1969. At the time, approximately 30,000 Salvadorans were living illegally in Honduras, refugees from the poverty and repression in El Salvador. Resentment among Hondurans against the Salvadoran squatters had been growing, and hostilities rose to a fever pitch in a soccer game played between the two countries in June 1969 in San Salvador. El Salvador launched a military strike against Honduras and, though the war was brief, more than 2,000 lives were lost.

Weekends see many Salvadorans heading for the beach in La Libertad where they can swim, laze around on the sand, walk out on the pier, and eat in one of the many open-air seaside restaurants.

A family gathers around to listen to the radio.

Only half the population owns a radio, while less than 10% has a television.

TELEVISION AND RADIO

In a small town on a Saturday night, it is not uncommon to see half the townspeople crowded around the doorway of a single small house lit by the bluish glow of a television—especially if a soccer match is on. Although El Salvador has several television stations, television sets are scarce, due to the widespread poverty and shortage of electricity. Only one in every 12 households has a set, and in rural areas television is almost non-existent. Those who do have a set sometimes offset the cost by charging their neighbors a few cents to watch it. Radios are more prevalent, and El Salvador has over 60 radio stations. Unlike its larger neighbors, El Salvador does not produce any of its own movies or television programs; most of them are imported from the United States or Mexico and are either dubbed into Spanish or given Spanish subtitles. Only city dwellers are lucky enough to have access to movie theaters.

STORYTELLING

A more common form of entertainment is storytelling. It does not cost anything, does not require any electrical gadgets or a knowledge of reading, and it can be used by mothers to entertain their children while carrying out household tasks. The same stories are heard all over the country, although they often have regional variations; common themes include the devil, who is typically disguised, and the struggle between good and evil. Among Indians, ancient legends about the creation of the world and of human beings are an important part of the culture, as well as a form of entertainment.

Folktales and legends are passed down through the generations by word of mouth.

DEVILISH FOLKTALES

The devil is a central figure in Salvadoran folktales. People try to avoid him out of fear that he will tempt them into giving their souls to him. One well-known story is *Justo Juez de la Noche*, or "Just Judge of the Night." The Just Judge is a tall man wearing a black suit who appears only at midnight. No one has ever seen his face, but his eyes are "like fire." He usually appears before lone travelers, especially in rural areas.

In one version of the story, a man named Julio is walking alone one night when he sees a very tall man blocking his path. The tall man, of course, is the Just Judge, although Julio does not know it. They walk and talk together for a long time. Suddenly, the Just Judge whips out his machete and tries to strike Julio with it, but Julio is experienced with a machete. He manages to strike the Just Judge with his own machete, but the blow has no effect. Instead, the Just Judge simply laughs with a laugh so loud that it can be heard from miles away. Julio sees the red eyes for the first time, and he runs away to avoid losing his soul, but he cannot escape losing his mind.

THE TOWN SQUARE

Small towns and villages in El Salvador, as in much of Latin America, are built around a central square, or plaza, which serves as the hub of the town's social, economic, and political life. The most important buildings, such as the church, the town hall, and the main stores border the plaza. The square is usually planted with trees, flowers, and shrubs, and is a popular center for playing games, relaxing, and socializing.

MUSIC AND DANCING

Salvadorans love getting together to sing, play music, and dance. The songs are often religious in nature, especially in church communities, or tell a story. Rock music from abroad is popular among young people and is played in nightclubs and discos in San Salvador, but everyone enjoys dancing to Latino music such as the lively *cumbia* and *salsa*, or the romantic *ranchera.*

THE AMERICAN INFLUENCE

American television programs, food brands, fashion trends, and leisure activities have made their presence felt throughout much of the world, and El Salvador is no exception. Baseball and skateboarding are popular pastimes. Fast-food restaurants such as McDonald's, Pizza Hut, and Dunkin' Donuts are easily found in the capital city of San Salvador and are much frequented by the young. Coca-Cola and Pepsi are the best-known brands of soft drinks, and blue jeans are worn by Salvadorans from all walks of life. U.S. situation comedies and series dominate the country's television channels, providing young Salvadorans with examples of the latest hairstyles, clothing, and verbal expressions. Pop songs from American chartbusting bands can be heard on many of El Salvador's radio stations.

FESTIVALS

THE INFLUENCE of El Salvador's long Catholic tradition combined with its Indian heritage have created a lively and colorful festival culture. The people of El Salvador celebrate several holidays as a nation, and in smaller groups through their towns and churches.

Most of the major festivals and holidays are religious and are the cause of particularly lengthy revelry—Christmas and Easter celebrations each last a full week. In addition, each city, village, and town has an annual festival for its patron saint, and some small towns embellish their town festivals with rich indigenous traditions.

HOLIDAYS AND FESTIVALS

New Year's Eve	December 31
New Year's Day	January 1
Palm Sunday	March/April (variable)
Easter Sunday	March/April (variable)
Labor Day	May 1
Day of the Vírgen de Fátima	May 13
Festival of El Salvador del Mundo	August 3–6
Independence Day	September 15
Columbus Day	October 12
All Souls' Day	November 2
Anniversary of 1st Call for Independence	November 5
Day of the Vírgen de Guadalupe	December 12
Christmas	December 25–31

Opposite: **The village of Santa Cruz Melada celebrates** *Carrera de Cintas*, **a festival of horses, with a variety of horse competitions.**

SEMANA SANTA

Holy Week, or *Semana Santa*, begins the week before Easter with Palm Sunday and is cause for grand celebrations within the Catholic Church. Catholics celebrate Palm Sunday, the day representing Jesus' entry into Jerusalem, by walking to Mass bearing flowers and palm branches. In some towns the streets are carpeted with flowers and lined with pictures of the Virgin Mary and Jesus.

All the stages of Christ's crucifixion and ascent into heaven are played out through dramatic ritual and elaborate celebration. The Last Supper is observed at Mass when the priest washes the feet of 12 men, just as the Bible says that Jesus washed the feet of his 12 disciples. On the Thursday, Friday, or Saturday of *Semana Santa*, they symbolically mourn the death of Jesus by giving up some personal comfort or luxury.

During *Semana Santa*, international surfing competitions are held at Zunzal, one of the best surfing beaches in Central America.

Semana Santa

On Good Friday, a group of people carry a cross and a life-size image of Jesus through town, while singing songs of his suffering. When the procession arrives at the church, it is met by four more people carrying an image of Jesus nailed to the cross. In the town of Izalco, the image of Jesus on the cross is so large that it takes 75 people to carry it. The image of Jesus is taken down from the cross at three o'clock in the afternoon. People wrap the image in white sheets and keep a candlelight vigil throughout the night at the church.

The tone of the entire day is very serious. Children are not supposed to run, because Judas ran after he betrayed Christ. Indeed, children generally do not play on Good Friday, nor do people travel, out of respect for Jesus' torturous journey to Calvary. *Semana Santa* is sincerely celebrated in El Salvador because so many people feel that it is symbolic of their own suffering and their hope for renewed life.

On Easter Saturday, people spend the day relaxing. They might sleep in late, then pack a lunch of tamales, watermelon, tortillas, and beans before spending the afternoon at the ocean or the nearest river. In the evening, they attend Mass. Outside the church, they circle around a bonfire; the priest uses the flames to light a candle, which in turn is used to light all the parishioners' candles. Then they enter the church in a lighted procession, which is meant to symbolize Christ before his resurrection from the dead.

The somber tone of *Semana Santa* ends on Easter Sunday, which is known as *Pascua*. People joyously celebrate by marching in a procession, again carrying the image of Jesus. They receive a blessing from the priest with holy water, and some people bring their animals to be blessed as well.

Semana Santa is especially beautiful in the smaller towns, where people celebrate the holiday to the fullest.

The Easter season begins on Ash Wednesday, the first day of Lent. Lent is observed for 40 days before Easter Sunday. During this time, people remember the sacrifice of Jesus through fasting and penitence.

CHRISTMAS

The season of Christmas begins a full month before Christmas Day, and runs on into January. As with *Semana Santa*, it is especially celebrated in the Catholic Church. Beginning on November 26, church members practice *posadas* ("po-SAH-das"), or "inns," taking statues of the Virgin Mary and Joseph from house to house every night until December 23, and spending a few hours singing, eating, and praying together at each house.

The holiday season reaches its climax on the night of December 24, which is called *La Noche Buena* ("lah NOH-chay BWEY-nah"), or "The Good Night." Everyone attends midnight Mass and then gathers at home to celebrate, often all night long. They drink and dance, open presents, and eat specially prepared foods such as tamales and turkey. Salvadoran children receive their gifts from *El Niño Dios* ("el NEE-nyo DEE-os"), or "Baby Jesus," on Christmas Eve.

People who can afford Christmas decorations usually decorate lavishly. They often have a Christmas tree, but more common is the nativity scene, or *nacimiento* ("na-see-mee-EN-toh"), whose statues or figurines are often life-size. *Nacimientos* can be very elaborate, with farms and villages and little roads leading to the manger. People with fewer resources decorate a single small branch or dry bush to create their Christmas tree. Decorations are not taken down until January 6, the Day of the Three Kings, or Epiphany, which commemorates the day that the Three Kings finally arrived to see the baby Jesus after following the Star of Bethlehem.

New Year's Eve, December 31, is another occasion for festive eating, drinking, and dancing; dinner typically consists of tamales and a roasted hen. But it can also be a rather melancholy holiday, filled with hugging and crying as people ask pardon of their loved ones for the sins of the past year and promise to behave better in the coming year.

Midnight Mass is called la misa del gallo, *or "the Rooster Mass," because people are still awake when the rooster crows.*

PATRON SAINTS' FESTIVALS

Because the Catholic Church has such a strong tradition in El Salvador, every city in the country has a patron saint, celebrated with a festival sometime during the year. The festivals usually last for an entire week and include a parade, soccer tournaments, and lots of eating, drinking, and dancing in the streets. The festivals are particularly colorful in Indian towns and villages; the celebrants dress up in their native costumes, with vivid plumage and colorful dress that is unique to their indigenous group, and their parade includes traditional indigenous dances and music. The biggest festival is held on August 6 for *El Salvador del Mundo*, or The Holy Savior of the World, patron saint of the whole country.

Townspeople honor their patron saint by carrying an image of the saint through the streets during the festival procession.

FOOD

THE STAPLE DIET of most Salvadorans, especially in rural areas, is beans, rice, and tortillas, mainly because they cannot afford much more. Despite the high starch content of these staple foods, most Salvadorans only get about two-thirds of the calories they need, and malnutrition is one of the leading causes of death among the rural population. Meat, poultry, and fish are a rare treat. The choice of food available to wealthier city dwellers is much wider, and includes a variety of vegetables, fruit, poultry, and seafood. San Salvador is well known for its Chinese, French, and Italian restaurants, and for the abundance of excellent seafood; shrimp, lobster, and swordfish are all caught daily off El Salvador's coast. *Pupusas* ("poo-POO-sas"), the national "fast food" of filled tortillas, are sold at food stalls, markets, and small restaurants throughout El Salvador.

Opposite: **Pupusas, a Salvadoran specialty, fry in a traditional iron pan.**

Left: **Live chickens ready for market in Santa Rosa.**

A Salvadoran worker prepares to eat a typical lunch of tortillas and beans.

THE TYPICAL SALVADORAN DIET

In rural areas, people eat breakfast before the sun comes up, so the men can start working in the fields very early. Breakfast, or *desayuno* ("de-sai-UN-o"), is a simple affair, consisting of coffee and a hot tortilla, which is sometimes diced and soaked in warm milk. Lunch, called *almuerzo* ("al-mu-AIR-so"), is the largest meal of the day. It typically consists of soup, with tortillas, rice, corn, or beans, and very occasionally meat, fish, or poultry. A typical family of six consumes less than two pounds of meat per month. As in most Latin American countries, lunch usually lasts for about two hours, giving field workers a chance to rest before resuming work until dark. Dinner, or the *cena* ("SAY-nah"), is often a lighter meal, consisting of vegetables, tortillas, and beans.

For urban Salvadorans, breakfast usually consists of coffee, bread, and fruit. The midday meal is often tortillas with rice and beans and is not necessarily the largest meal of the day. Urban Salvadorans are not typically able to

LESS THAN NUTRITIOUS

The average Salvadoran consumes 2,306 calories per day, almost the full recommended daily requirement, but gets only 55.2 grams of protein, about half the amount consumed by the average American. Most poor Salvadorans, of course, get far less than the national average. This lack of protein leads to serious nutritional problems, especially among pregnant women in rural parts of the country.

TORTILLA MAKING

Making tortillas is considered to be the exclusive task of women. A woman starts making the day's supply of tortillas for her family early in the morning. The traditional method of making tortillas from scratch and by hand is still used by the typical rural woman. First she must soak or boil the hard kernels of ripe corn in a mixture of water and white lime, which turns the corn into a starchy dough. She uses a handstone called a *mano* ("MAH-no") to grind the dough on a grinding stone, called a *metate* ("may-TAH-tay"). Then she kneads the dough by hand, slapping it back and forth between her hands until it forms a thin, round patty. When the tortillas are ready to be cooked, she fries them on a hot griddle, called a *comal* ("co-MAHL").

take a siesta in the middle of the day, unlike many other Latin Americans, although some shops do close for an hour or two at lunchtime. Families usually eat the evening meal together, which may include soup or vegetables, beans, rice, tortillas, and fish or meat. City supermarkets also provide a variety of processed foods imported from abroad.

DRINKS

Although coffee is El Salvador's primary export, the coffee served in El Salvador is often instant. Whether it is instant or brewed, it tends to be

weak and bland. Salvadorans often dilute it with barley juice, and in rural areas, the taste is further spoiled by the necessity of adding bleach to the water to help prevent cholera. The most common cold drinks are *gaseosas* ("ga-say-OH-sas"), or sodas, and *refrescos* ("ray-fres-KOS"), which are fruit juices mixed with sugar and water. Locally brewed beer and spirits are also popular. Tic-Tack, a particularly strong spirit made from sugarcane, has been nicknamed the "national liquor of El Salvador." Like vodka, it is colorless, but has an even higher alcohol content.

Above: **Bottles of Tic-Tack, the national liquor, stand on a supermarket shelf.**

Right: **In rural El Salvador, coffee is ground by hand.**

IN THE KITCHEN

Kitchens in rural houses are usually located outside the house, either in a separate building or under a roof extending from the house. The women cook over a fire, or on a raised cement platform oven with a hollow center for the fire, over which they put a grill or griddle made of clay or metal. They must walk to the nearest river or stream to fetch water, which they ration carefully throughout the day for their cooking and cleaning purposes.

Middle- and upper-class families, on the other hand, usually have at least one maid to help with cooking and cleaning. The maid will often do the shopping, although the *señora* ("se-NYO-rah"), or lady of the house, will usually prepare the list for her, and may even accompany her to the market. The *señora* also directs the daily menu, but the maid does most of the cooking. The kitchens in these houses are modern compared to rural kitchens, but they typically lack appliances such as dishwashers and washing machines because the maid cleans the dishes and often washes the clothes by hand.

A typical grocery store in a small town offers a limited range of goods, and the food is not refrigerated.

MARKETS

The traditional open-air market in El Salvador is crowded with close-set stalls offering a wide variety of goods: hot tortillas and tamales, handmade baskets, colorful flowers, fresh fruit and vegetables, live chickens or pigs, and shoes, clothes, hammocks, and dishes. The air is full of rich aromas and noisy bargaining by women carrying netted handbags or large wicker baskets on their heads to hold their daily purchases. Shoppers thread their way through row upon row of fresh produce including bananas, mangoes, melons, carrots, corn, avocados, cabbages, tomatoes, peppers, garlic, and potatoes. In the larger cities, modern supermarkets have supplanted some of the open-air markets, providing shoppers with an array of refrigerated, processed, and canned foods.

A modern supermarket in San Salvador.

SALVADORAN SPECIALTIES

One of the most delicious and interesting foods is the *pupusa* ("poo-POO-sah"), which is unique to El Salvador. *Pupusas* are small, thick corn tortillas filled with sausage, cheese, or beans and served hot, with salad or salsa. They are sold in *pupuserías* ("poo-poo-say-REE-ah") all over El Salvador.

Tamales—steamed rolls of cornmeal stuffed with shredded meat, peppers, and corn and wrapped in corn husks—are another popular food, common to many Central American countries. Tamales take a great deal of time to prepare and are considered a dish for special occasions.

A favorite soup in El Salvador is *sopa de pata* ("SOH-pah deh PAH-tah"), or "hoof soup," made from the hoof of a cow or an ox, with vegetables, and sometimes with beef tripe. *Sopa de pata* is made year-round, but it is especially popular during holidays and at family gatherings.

It takes an experienced hand to make *pupusas*, a Salvadoran specialty of stuffed tortillas.

PUPUSAS: A UNIQUE SALVADORAN FOOD

This recipe makes 12 cheese *pupusas*.

3 cups *masa harina* (cornmeal, found in grocery stores)
2 teaspoons salt
1¹/₂ cups warm water

¹/₂ lb Monterrey Jack cheese, grated
¹/₄ green bell pepper, minced
vegetable oil for frying

In a large bowl, combine *masa harina* with salt and water. Mix into a pliable dough. Cover with plastic wrap and refrigerate for one hour.

Mix cheese with green pepper. Set aside.

Prepare the *cortido* (see below). Set aside.

Remove dough from the refrigerator. Divide into six balls, then divide each ball again into four balls. Place a piece of plastic wrap on a flat surface. Place one ball of dough on top of the plastic and cover with a second piece of plastic. Use a rolling pin to flatten it into a circle about three inches in diameter. Do the same with the remaining balls of dough.

Remove the plastic wrap from the dough and place about two teaspoons of the cheese mixture in the center of the circle, leaving a ¹/₄-inch border. Cover with a second circle of dough and seal by pressing the edges together. Repeat with remaining balls of dough.

Heat a thin layer of vegetable oil in a large skillet and cook a few *pupusas* at a time over moderate heat for 2–3 minutes per side, or until they are golden brown. Drain on paper towels and place in a warm oven while cooking the remaining *pupusas*. Serve immediately with *cortido*.

Cortido
1 medium onion, thinly sliced
1¹/₂ cups shredded green cabbage
1 large carrot, peeled and shredded
3 cloves garlic, minced

¹/₄ cup apple cider vinegar
2 teaspoons dried oregano
salt and pepper to taste

Combine salad ingredients in a bowl and mix well. Season with salt and pepper and let stand for 30 minutes at room temperature before serving.

Salvadoran girls learn from an early age how to perfect the art of gently patting the pupusas back and forth between their hands until they are perfectly ready to be cooked on the griddle.

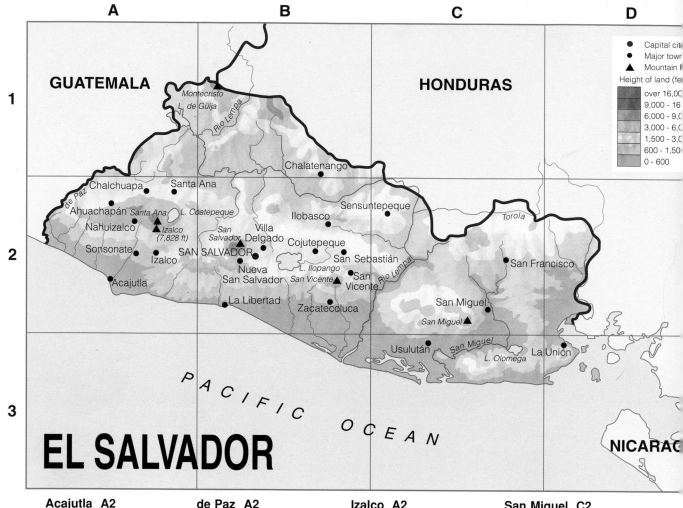

EL SALVADOR

Acajutla A2
Ahuachapán A2

Chalatenango B1
Chalchuapa A2
Cojutepeque B2

de Paz A2

Guatemala A1

Honduras C1

Ilobasco B2

Izalco A2
Izalco (mountain) A2

L. Coatepeque A2
L. de Güijia A1
L. Ilopango B2
L. Olomega C3
La Libertad B2
La Union C3

Montecristo (Mt.) A1

Nahuizalco A2
Nicaragua D3
Nueva San Salvador B2

Pacific Ocean A3

Rio Lempa B1, C2

San Francisco C2

San Miguel C2
San Miguel (Mt.) C2
San Miguel River C3
San Salvador A2
San Salvador (Mt.) B2
San Sebastián B2
San Vicente B2
San Vicente (Mt.) B2
Santa Ana A2
Santa Ana (Mt.) A2
Sensuntepeque B2
Sonsonate A2

Torola River C2

Usulután C3

Villa Delgado B2

Zacatecoluca B2

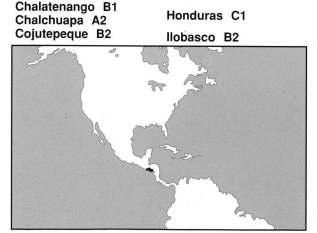

QUICK NOTES

AREA
8,260 square miles

POPULATION
5,418,000 (1991 estimate)

POPULATION DENSITY
666 people per square mile

CAPITAL
San Salvador

MAJOR CITIES
San Salvador, Santa Ana, San Miguel

MAJOR RIVER
Lempa River

MAJOR LAKES
Lake Ilopango, Lake Coatepeque,
Lake de Güija

NATIONAL FLOWER
Izote

NATIONAL TREE
Maquilishuat

HIGHEST POINT
Izalco (7,828 feet)

OFFICIAL LANGUAGE
Spanish

MAJOR RELIGION
Catholic

CURRENCY
Colón (c8.8 = $1)

MAIN EXPORTS
Coffee, textiles & garments, sugar, shrimp

LEADERS IN POLITICS
José Napoleón Duarte—Former leader of
the moderate Christian Democratic
Party; president of El Salvador 1984–
1988

Alfredo Cristiani—Former leader of the
rightwing ARENA party; president of El
Salvador 1989–1994

LEADERS IN THE ARTS
Manlio Argueta (writer)
María Mendoza de Baratta (composer)
Roque Dalton (writer)
Alvaro Menén Desleal (dramatist)
Fernando Llort (painter)
Waldo Chávez Velasco (dramatist)
Italo López Vallecillos (dramatist)
José Mejía Vides (painter)

GLOSSARY

coup Removal of a government, illegally and by force.

curandero ("cur-ahn-DE-roh") Indian witch doctor or healer.

Cuscatlán Indian name for the region that now includes El Salvador.

junta Small group ruling a country, especially after a coup and before a legal government has been elected.

matanza ("mah-TAN-zah") Massacre or slaughter.

mesones ("may-SON-ays") Single-story buildings, usually rundown, consisting of a connected series of small, individual dwellings, surrounding a common courtyard.

mestizo ("mes-TEE-so") Person of mixed European and Indian ancestry.

oligarchy A small group of people exercising political control, usually for corrupt and selfish purposes.

padrinos ("pa-DREE-nos") Godparents (*padrino* and *madrino* = godfather and godmother).

pupusa ("poo-POO-sah") Thick corn tortilla filled with beans, meat, or cheese; special dish of El Salvador.

pupusería ("poo-poo-say-REE-ah") Small restaurant or food stall where *pupusas* are sold.

tugurios ("tu-GU-ryos") Shantytowns.

BIBLIOGRAPHY

Manlio Argueta: *One Day of Life*, Vintage International, New York, 1983.

Faren Maree Bachelis: *El Salvador*, Children's Press, Chicago, 1990.

Tom Barry: *El Salvador: A Country Guide*, Albuquerque, The Inter-Hemispheric Education Resource Center, New Mexico, 1990.

Nathan A. Haverstock, *El Salvador in Pictures*, Lerner Publications, Minneapolis, 1987.

Nancy Keller, Tom Broasnahan, and Rob Rachowiecki: *Central America*, Lonely Planet Publications, Berkeley, 1992.

INDEX

INDEX

INDEX